GERANIUM
PINK BOUQUET

Caption to front end paper
Zonal Pelargoniums var. Pink Bouquet
Photo H. Smith

Geraniums and Pelargoniums

Geraniums
and
Pelargoniums

H. G. WITHAM-FOGG

JOHN GIFFORD LTD
LONDON : 1975

John Gifford Ltd
125 Charing Cross Road
London, WC2H 0EB

ISBN 0 7071 0500 5

Text set in Times Roman and
printed in Great Britain by the Hope Burgess Group.
Bound by Redwood Burn, Esher

Contents

	List of coloured illustrations	11
	List of black and white illustrations	12
	Foreword	13
	Acknowledgements	14
1	Introducing the Geranium	15
2	The uses of Flowers and Foliage	25
3	Cultural requirements	34
4	Propagation	39
5	Bedding out	51
6	Pots, Tubs, Baskets and Window Boxes	56
7	Zonal Pelargoniums	66
8	Regal Pelargoniums	77
9	Ivy-leafed varieties	87
10	Variegated-leafed Geraniums	93
11	Scented-leafed Geraniums	105
12	Dwarf Geraniums	112
13	Unusual varieties	118
14	Pelargonium species	124
15	Flowering and Care in Winter	130
16	The true Hardy Geranium	133
17	Some Geranium diseases	142
18	Pests and their treatment	149
	Appendix	152
	Index	154

List of coloured illustrations

A variegated-leafed Geranium, Mrs. Pollock	15
Blaze Geraniums	19
Variegated-leafed Geranium, Mrs. Henry Cox	22
Zonal Pelargonium, Pink Bouquet	23
Irenes as cut-flowers	26
Deacon Bonanza	27
Hanging Basket	30
Pot and paving	31
Various Dwarf Geraniums in a greenhouse	34
Pollination	39
The potting bench	43
A border of Dwarf Geraniums	51
Ready for planting out	54
Window Box	58
Wall basket	59
Geranium in pots	62
Hanging Basket	63
Pelargonium, Carousel	66
Pelargonium, Decorator	67
Irene Geranium Penny	71
Zonal Geranium, Paul Crampel	75
Regal Pelargonium, Carisbrooke	78
Regal Pelargonium, Mrs. E. Hickman	79
The Rembrandt Collection	82
The Vandyke Collection	83
Ivy-leafed Geranium, Beryl Wood	87
Ivy-leafed Pelargonium, Balcon Rouge	90
Ivy-leafed Pelargonium, Mme. Crousse	91
Pelargonium, Golden Harry Hieover	94
Pelargonium, Caroline Schmidt	95
Fragrans Variegata	99
Variegated-leafed Pelargonium, Mme. Salleron	103
Pelargonium Denticulatum	107
Geranium Crispum	111
Dwarf Geraniums	114
Dwarf Geraniums	115

List of black and white illustrations

Zonal Pelargonium – Pink Bouquet   *Front end paper*

Fig. 1   Pelargonium inquinans   17

Fig. 2a Semi-double flowers   52

Fig. 2b Fully double flowers   52

Fig. 3   Typical single flowers of Zonal Pelargoniums   61

Fig. 4   Fancy-leafed zonal Geraniums   98

Fig. 5   Different forms of scented-leafed Geraniums   106

Fig. 6   Geraniums of unusual shape   119

Fig. 7   Pelargonium ferulaceum   125

Fig. 8   Pelargonium slenopelatum   127

Ivy-leafed Pelargonium – Balcon Rouge   *Back end paper*

Foreword

IN WRITING this book Mr. Witham Fogg has rendered a great service not only to horticulturists generally, but also to the ever-increasing ranks of enthusiastic amateur pelargonium growers. In comparatively recent years, there have been several works presented which would appear to fall into two categories, one sketchy and slightly informative, and the other erudite and lengthy with references etc. I therefore welcome this work as a nicely balanced and up-to-date book.

During my own research I have found that the major problem has been that not enough knowledge has been recorded. If only people would write down their successes and indeed their failures, in the field of cultivations, then we, the seekers of 'Geranium Truths', would be greatly helped towards our goal. I therefore commend this book to you as a tremendous step forward in the hopes and aspirations of all pelargonium enthusiasts.

1964   ANTHONY C. AYTON
Former Chairman of The Geranium Society

MR. WITHAM FOGG has been a member of the British Pelargonium and Geranium Society since its earliest days and a large number of his various editions on the Pelargonium and Geranium have been sold to our members and others.

There is no doubt of the popularity of his works which have contributed greatly to the knowledge of the plant as now known by the horticultural public.

All of us who are so keenly devoted to the plant are deeply indebted to Mr. Fogg for the tremendous amount of work he has put into his books. I know that with this much wanted revised edition there will be big sales around the world.

Our Author member has been of great value to our Society because of the increasing demand for books on the subject.

1974   HENRY J. WOOD
Secretary of the British Pelargonium and Geranium Society

Acknowledgements

Since the publication of my handbook, *Geranium Growing,* almost twenty years ago, I have received letters regarding geraniums from all five continents, proving that the interest in these plants is world wide. In writing the present volume, I have been fortunate in obtaining help and advice from professional and amateur growers, both in this country and abroad.

I am especially grateful to Mr. A. C. Ayton, the specialist grower, for his readiness to help with descriptions.

To the Botanical Society of South Africa and to Mrs. F. M. Isaacs (nee Leighton) I offer thanks for permission to quote from an article on the difference between pelargoniums and geraniums. Thanks are due to Messrs. Wilson Bros., of Roachdale, Indiana, U.S.A., for photographs and assistance in determining the grouping of the perfumed leaved varieties. Mr. F. G. Read has also been generous in giving information.

I have been helped by descriptions given in the catalogue of Mr. Holmes C. Miller, of Los Altos, California, who has been additionally kind in providing photographs. Mr. Fred A. Bode, of the Geranium Gardens, Escondido, California, has been extremely helpful in giving information at all times and providing photographs.

I am grateful to the following individuals and firms for providing photographs: H. Smith, F. G. Read, Holmes C. Miller, H. Bagust, Wyck Hill Gardens, H. Woolman, and W. Blom Ltd., while Mr. H. J. Wood, Secretary of The British Geranium and Pelargonium Society, has been kind enough to write a Foreword.

A Variegated-leafed Geranium, 'Mrs. Pollock'   *Photo H. Bagust*

1 Introducing the Geranium

ALMOST ALL of us, as children or adults, have under one circumstance or another, become acquainted with the geranium. This plant has been in cultivation for about 300 years and although there have been periods when it has been ignored by both the professional and amateur gardener, it has regularly returned to popularity. It is more loved today than it has ever been, not only in Britain but in many other parts of the world.

There are many reasons for the popularity of the geranium, although first perhaps, we ought to make sure to what plant we are referring, since there is considerable confusion as to the connection between the names 'geranium' and 'pelargonium'.

The name 'geranium' has its origin in antiquity, having been used by Dioscorides, who lived in the days of Nero and Pliny. As I wrote in *Geranium Growing*, a handbook published first in 1955, the name defined by Linnaeus in his *Species Plantarum* of 1753 comprised three distinct genera, viz. geranium proper or 'Crane's Bill', pelargonium or 'Stork's Bill', and erodium or 'Heron's

Bill'. These names are descriptive of the shape of the fruit. The genera pelargonium and erodium were named by a French botanist, L'Heritier in 1788. The true geranium is a cosmopolitan genus of which about eight species are native to South Africa. It is seldom cultivated as an ornamental garden plant in South Africa although a number of introduced species, and a few species of erodium as well, occur as weeds.

Pelargoniums are distinguished from geraniums by their irregular flowers, by the nectariferous spur which adheres to the pedicel, and by the shape of the fruit.

Pelargonium, though largely South African in origin, extends to Madagascar and up to the east coast of Africa to Arabia and western India. There are species in Australia and on Tristan da Cunha. From the South African species have arisen all the manifold varieties of pelargonium and so-called 'ivy-leaved and zonal geraniums' of horticulture.

Some botanical writers of the early nineteenth century insisted on following the usage of Linnaeus, and declined to accept the new name pelargonium. Among these was H. C. Andrews whose prolific writing and whose popularity among gardeners of his day have probably had much to do with the persistence of the name geranium for a large section of the garden varieties of pelargonium. In the preface to his monumental work on the geranium published about 1820 Andrews says: 'If such generic divisions, that is the splitting of Linnaeus's genus into geranium, erodium and pelargonium were generally adopted, the approach to botanic science would be so choked up with ill-shaped, useless lumber that, like a castle in a fairy tale, guarded by hideous dwarfs, none but a botanic Quixote would attempt investigation'. The genus pelargonium is, nevertheless, accepted by botanists today—quixotic or otherwise.

Among the hardy plants which were collected by early visitors to the Cape and which survived the voyage to Europe, was *Pelargonium triste*, a humble plant of the sandy flats and lower slopes. It is a low growing rather inconspicuous plant, which attracts little attention from modern gardeners.

Thomas Johnson in his edition of *Gerard's Herball* published in 1633, refers to it as follows: 'There is of late brought into his kingdome, and to our knowledge by the industry of Mr. John Tradescant, another more rare and no less beautiful than any of the former, hee had it by the name of *Geranium indicum noctu odoratum*; this hath not as yet been written of by any that I know; therefore I will give you the description thereof, but cannot as yet give you the figure, because I omitted the taking thereof the last years and it has not as yet come to his perfection. The leaves are larger, being almost a foot long, composed of sundry little leaves of an unequal bigness, set upon a thick and stiff middle rib and these leaves are much divided and cut in . . . they are thicke, green and somewhat hairie: the stalks is thicke and some cubit high; at the top of each branch upon foot stalkes some inch long grows some eleven or twelve floures, and each of the floures consisteth of five round pointed leaves of a yellowish colour with a large blacke purple spot in the middle of each leafe as it were painted, which gives the floure a great deal of beauty; and it also hath a good smell. I did see it in floure about the end of July 1632 being the first time that it floured with the owner thereof. We may fitly call it Sweet Indian Storksbill or painted Storksbill; and in Latin *Geranium indicum odoratum flore maculato*'.

16   The inclusion of the word *indicum* shows that, as with a number of other

Fig. 1. *Pelargonium inquinans*

Cape plants taken to Europe by ships returning from the East, *Pelargonium triste* was thought to have come from India or the Indies. John Tradescant's garden was in Lambeth, South London.

In 1635 Parkinson wrote of *P. triste*: 'The flowers smell very swette like Muske in the night onely and not at all in the day time as refusing the Sunnes influence but delighteth in the Moones appearance'.

The next reference to this species is in 1688 in Florens Schuyls Catalogue of the Leyden Botanic Gardens. It is listed among the introductions from the Cape of Good Hope. When Paul Hermann published his catalogue of these gardens in 1687 the number of 'geraniums' from the Cape had risen to ten. Hermann had visited the Cape about 1672 and tells us that he found *P. cucullatum* growing at the foot of Table Mountain.

From Aiton's catalogue of the plants cultivated at the Royal Botanic Gardens, Kew, published in 1759, we learn that it was introduced in 1690 by Mr. Bentick.

With the advent of the more spectacular and colourful pelargoniums, *P. triste* seems to have fallen from favour, although it was still grown in European gardens. A coloured picture appeared in Curtis Botanical Magazine in 1814.

17

During the eighteenth century indeed, many of our pelargoniums found their way into European gardens. Among these was *P. inquinans*, one of the progenitors of the many types of red 'geranium'. It first made its appearance in literature in the *Hortus Elthamensis* of Dillenius in 1732 and Aiton says that it was cultivated as early as 1714 by Bishop Compton, a Bishop of London who seems to have shown a marked interest in botany in general and in South African plants in particular. He acquired, when on a visit to Holland, a Codex which probably included some of the Claudius drawings from the Cape (or copies of them).

The forerunner of the 'ivy-leaved geranium', *P. peltatum*, was introduced into Holland in 1700 by Willem Adriaan van der Stel. The seeds came from the 'region of Heycoon'. Seeds of *P. zonale* were sent in the same year from the 'region of the Attaqua'.

With these, and others, established in gardens during the seventeenth and eighteenth centuries, hybrids began to arise.

Both names, geraniums and pelargonium, are well known to most gardeners, although it is not always realized what are their differences. Both belong to the natural order *Geraniaceae* and the confusion in the use of the two names is not altogether surprising. The true geranium is to be found in several of our native species long admired as wild flowers, one of which is the Herb Robert, *Geranium robertianum*, with its pretty pink flowers, so frequently seen growing alongside country lanes and roads. There are a number of other wildlings but we need not consider them now. The cultivated section of the hardy geraniums will be dealt with later.

The word pelargonium comes from pelargos which literally means a stork, in allusion to the beak-like form of the seed pod. Similarity in the derivation of the names geranium and pelargonium – Cranesbill and Storksbill – is sufficient to indicate the reason for the confusion and ambiguity which often occur in the use of these names. Furthermore, another part of the *geraniaceae*, the erodiums which are also referred to later, are commonly known as Heronsbills.

However, there *are* botanical differences between the geranium and pelargonium. Simply put, we may say that whereas the petals of the former are regular in shape, the flowers being without spurs and having ten stamens, the pelargonium has irregular petals, often only two or three upper ones, the remainder being very small, and its flowers are spurred with not more than five stamens.

The well-known bedding eranium so often seen in many brilliant coloured varieties, of which 'Paul Crampel' has long been best known, is, strictly speaking, *Pelargonium zonale*. The original species itself had, and has, in its native habitat of South Africa, foliage with a dark horseshoe zone which accounts for the designation zonale.

Many of the modern varieties of the species have entirely unmarked leaves, without even a trace of the darker zoning, although they are true Pelargonium zonale hybrids. Here it must be said that the tremendous number of zonal pelargoniums now in cultivation have come, not entirely from *zonale* itself, but from that species and *P. inquinans*. It would appear evident that much of the bolder type of flower, as well as the size of the truss and the rather succulent appearance of the foliage, is due to the influence of *P. inquinans*. It is also probable that the absence of the zonal or horseshoe markings in many varities is due to the same parent.

18

The Show or Regal pelargonium is *P. domesticum* which has been grown in Britain for very many years. In America they are known as Martha or Lady Washingtons, and in Germany as Edelpelargonien. These have very large blooms in many striking colours and are really best when grown under glass. Few if any of the Regals will flower during the winter, though the zonals frequently do. They are, however, admirable for giving a wealth of colour from the early summer onwards, when they frequently appear as pot plants in the house and never fail to attract attention when exhibited at Flower Shows. In addition, in sheltered gardens they may be used out of doors with great advantage if given the background of a low wall or fence. As cut flowers too, they are occasionally used for bouquets and decorative purposes, when the beautifully marked and blotched flowers give a charming, exotic display without appearing gaudy or flamboyant. It will be easily realized why regal and show varieties were so popular a century ago, for their richly coloured blooms of substance have that comfortable, peaceful look characteristic of that time.

In spite of the hardiness of the true geranium, which can be used in the rock garden and border, as indicated in Chapter XVI, the true pelargoniums, whether they be the *P. zonale*, *P. domesticum* or *P. peltatum* (ivy-leaved) varieties, are much more popular and showy.

As we shall see later, many species and hybrids are grown for their scented leaves and some because of their attractively coloured foliage. Some have

Blaze Geraniums   *Photo Wilson Bros., U.S.A.*

deeply lobed cut-edged leaves, others are shallowly lobed. There are low growing, thick stemmed species and others that are tall and slender. Although the majority of pelargoniums have fibrous roots there are a few which are tuberous-rooted.

With few exceptions, the wild species are natives of South Africa. In their natural habitats they hybridize to some extent, but in cultivation extensive and intensive hybridization has taken place. Sometimes this has been by plan, often by chance, but these crossings have obscured the origin of many widely grown pelargoniums. This has resulted in the origin and identity of some of the cultivated varieties becoming confused. At various times, attempts have been made to clarify some of the major problems of naming. These efforts have brought to light previous errors of identification and in some cases, the need for a change of name, although, where a name has been in use for a very long time, this is not always easy to effect.

In an article by Harold E. Moore, Junior, in *Baileyana*, Volume 3, No. 1. we may find an example of the confusion of names. This concerns *Pelargonium citriodorum*, a scented-leaved species. There are two uses of this name, as Thomas Sprague has pointed out in the 'Kew Bulletin' for 1922, page 155, and our garden material should be called *pelargonium × citrosum*.

Pelargonium citriodorum (*Cavanilles*) *Martius* was based on geranium citriodorum, illustrated and described by Cavanilles in the first volume of his '*Icones et Descriptiones Plantarum*' (1791). When Martius transferred Cavanilles' name to pelargonium in '*Plantarum Horti Academici Erlangensis*' (1814), it became the first *Pelargonium citriodorum*. Although considered a synonym, or at least a very similar derivative, of *P. acerifolium*, it pre-empts the use of a name commonly applied in gardens to the plant mentioned below.

The usual horticultural material bearing the name *P. citriodorum* is a hybrid derived from *P. crispum* and has a long history in cultivation. At the beginning of the nineteenth century, Henry Andrews illustrated a variety of hybrid garden form under the name *Geranium citriodorum*. Since there was already the different *Geranium citriodorum* mentioned above, Andrews' name was inadmissible and has no botanical standing. Unfortunately, the name appears to have been widely disseminated along with plants. In *Hortus Breiterianus* (1817), Breiter listed *Pelargonium citriodorum* without description and cited another name, *P. citrosum Voigt*, as a synonym. Similar plants must have been grown at Ratisbon (Regensburg) in Bavaria, for in 1828 Schrank gave the first description and used the name *Pelargonium citriodorum* in the second volume of *Sylloge Plantarum Novarum*, a work dealing primarily with plants grown at Ratisbon, and published in that city.

This later name cannot be accepted under our present code of botanical nomenclature because it duplicated one already known. In 1922 Sprague, taking the name from Breiter's list, suggested the use of *P. × citrosum Voigt* to supplant Schrank's *P. citriodorum*. Although the name must date from Sprague's application of it in 1922, and not from its use as a synonym in 1817, it may be taken up for the *P. citriodorum* of horticulture.

The situation is further confused by the uncertainty of identity between today's plants and those of the last century. It would be preferable to use fancy names rather than the poorly defined *P. × citrosum*. Although the latter is listed in *Hortus III*, the clone most commonly grown as *P. citriodorum* will be noted simply as Pelargonium 'Prince of Orange'.

Introducing the Geranium

In summary then:

1. *P. citriodorum* (*Cavanilles*) *Martius* is a synonym of the earlier *P. acerifolium L'Heritier ex Aiton*, a species not certainly known in cultivation in the United States.

2. *P.* × *citrosum Voigt ex Sprague* should replace the name *P. citriodorum Schrank* of horticulture, or the clones believed to be of this alliance may be listed simply by their fancy names, such as pelargonium 'Prince of Orange'.

In Volume 3, Number 2 of *Baileyana*, a quarterly journal of horticultural taxonomy, published by the Bailey Hortorium, Cornell University, New York, the same Harold E. Moore, Junior, gives a helpful key to groups of pelargonium species. Since this is so helpful, it is repeated here, by permission, although not in full detail.

Grouping of species according to leaf-characters:
A. Leaves sweet, spicy or pungent-scented.
B. Leaves white—hairy underneath.
C. Leaves pinnate or pinnately lobed.
D. Leaves palinately lobed.
E. Leaves entire or shallowly lobed–rounded in outline.

Grouping of species according to stem characters:
A. Stems absent.
B. Stem strongly angled.
C. Stem swollen at the joints.
D. Stem spiny.
E. Stem thick, succulent, often gnarled and misshapen.

The pelargonium is very free in producing new forms and this is one of the reasons for the confusion which has arisen in regard to naming and classification. In addition, different names are used in other countries for the same variety. For example, in the United States 'Skelly's Pride' is known as 'Jean' and many other zonals and regals have entirely different titles.

However, both the British and American Geranium Societies are fully aware of the muddle that there is in nomenclature, and they have taken steps to establish an authoritative means of registration. A system of naming is now in operation, whereby proposed names for new introductions are first submitted for approval instead of anyone giving a name to any plant of their choice, however similar it may be to a variety already in commerce.

The British Pelargonium and Geranium Society maintains a nomenclature sub-committee which continues the work of ensuring the correct naming of all new cultivars, in addition to ensuring correct naming of older varieties, and the unravelling of synonyms.

This committee has now issued an invaluable detailed check list. The method of classification adopted is given under the following nine headings, although there are many sub-sections grouped under these same headings:

A. Zonal pelargoniums.
B. Regal pelargoniums.
C. Ivy-leaved pelargoniums.
D. Hybrid ivy-leaved pelargoniums.
E. Scented-leaved pelargoniums.

F. Unique pelargoniums.
G. Angel pelargoniums.
H. Species pelargoniums.
J. Primary hybrids.

The following is a condensed resumé of the rules concerning the naming of plants, now generally accepted in all countries, and known as the *International Code of Nomenclature for Cultivated Plants* (1952):

1. The term 'variety' (abbreviated var. or v.) is reserved for those forms which are known to occur in the wild and which have names in Latin.
2. The term 'cultivar' (abbreviated cv.) is applied to those special forms which have originated or are maintained only in cultivation.
3. The name and descriptions must be published in a dated catalogue, technical work or periodical.
4. No cultivar names should be in Latin.
5. A cultivar name should be used only once in the same genus.
6. A cultivar name should consist of not more than two words.
7. When naming cultivars after persons, avoid such forms as 'Mr.', 'Mrs.', 'Sir' or first name initials: thus, 'Mary Brown' is acceptable but not 'Mrs. Mary Brown', 'M. Brown', 'Mrs. Brown' or 'Mrs. M. Brown'.

Variegated-leafed Geranium, Mrs. Henry Cox   *Photo H. Bagust*

Zonal Pelargoniums, Pink Bouquet   *Photo H. Smith*

8. The articles 'A' and 'The', unless required by linguistic custom, should be avoided; thus 'La Rochelle' is acceptable but not 'The Colonel'.
9. Abbreviations for personal and geographical names should be avoided; thus 'William Thomas' and 'Mount Kisco' are acceptable but not 'Wm. Thomas' and 'Mt. Kisco'.

The name of a genus should not be used as a name of a garden variety. *Pelargonium carnation*, for example, is an undesirable name.

Registration will not be restricted to new introductions. In fact, the success of the programme depends in large measure on the registration of established cultivars. The applicant will be required to provide a specimen of the subject plant. These specimens will be used in assembling an authentic collection of registered plants to provide a direct method of identification and comparison.

In the early part of the nineteenth century–1805 to be exact–there was published in London a *Monograph of the Genus Geranium* and in 1820 R. Sweet published his *Geraniaceae*, a comprehensive work in five volumes, which is still regarded as a standard guide to the earlier pelargonium species and hybrids, many of which are now unobtainable. The hand-coloured illustrations of these species make the book extremely valuable, in spite of the fact that it does not contain the better known zonal geraniums of the present time. 23

Since the last war a number of practical books have been published both in this country and the United States, a sure sign of the increasing popularity of the geranium.

In one of his novels, *Laughter on the Stairs*, Beverley Nichols says in his own amusing way:

'Geraniums to me are a sort of test flower, for long experience has told me that people who do not like geraniums have something morally unsound about them. Sooner or later you will find them out, you will discover that they drink or steal or speak sharply to cats. Never trust a man or woman who is not passionately devoted to geraniums.'

While technically it may be correct to refer to them as 'pelargoniums', to most people the bedding or zonal, the ivy-leaved, the variegated and scented-leaved varieties are popularly known as geraniums, and no doubt they will continue to be thought of under that name.

The British Geranium Society founded in 1951, is continually extending its influence through its publications and annual shows. The annual subscription is £1 and this society is worthy of the support of all who have an interest in the attractive and versatile 'geranium'.

If you would like to know more about the society, write to The Hon. Secretary, The British Pelargonium and Geranium Society, 129 Aylesford Avenue, Beckenham, Kent, BR3 3RX. The society supplies, and benefits from the sale of books on all aspects of pelargonium culture.

2 The uses of Flowers and Foliage

AS A CUT FLOWER for decorative purposes, the geranium has never had the publicity it deserves. This, of course, is largely due to the flower not being used as freely as it might by florists. Now, through the activities of the British Pelargonium and Geranium Society, more use of cut geranium flowers for decoration *is* being made. In this, all lovers of the flower can help, for certain varieties, including the so-called Rosebud varieties, can be used by ladies for their personal adornment. It should be remembered that, picked when young and just opening, and with a tiny spot of florist's gum dropped into the base of the petals, the flowers will retain their freshness and charm for many hours. The right sized, small heads of flowers can be tucked into the hair and a suitable shade of colour can be selected to match almost any sort or shade of make-up.

They can also be worn as sprays with green or variegated foliage. The leaves of varieties such as 'Caroline Schmidt', which are grey-green with straw-coloured edges, 'Harry Hieover', gold with bronze zone, and 'Flower of Spring', lavender-green, pale yellow edge, are all useful for this purpose. As for the flowers to go with them, what could be better than those rose-like varieties, 'Pink Rambler' and 'Red Rambler', which are included in the Rosebud geraniums referred to above.

Many other varities can be used, the choice depending on what is available and the occasion for which the display is needed. They look well too, in many of the modern floral decorations. In her book *How to do the Flowers*, Mrs. Constance Spry includes a delightful photograph in which regal pelargoniums are used in conjunction with Lily of the Valley, irises, lilac and dicentra, to form an arresting yet simple display.

Without much difficulty, it is possible to use pelargoniums in flower arrangements for the greater part of the year. This, of course, is because of the continuous flowering capabilities of some of the zonal and regal varieties. Flowers from the two sections go very well together, since the light, delicate, rather spreading habit of the regals give the necessary contrast to the formal-looking, solid zonals. The ivy-leaved and scented-leaved varieties can be included, not particularly on account of their flowers, but rather because of their attractive foliage, which can be made to hang into almost any position.

All flowers should be cut before they are fully open, and should there be any objection to cutting, on account of the removal of part of the stems needed to set off the flowers, there is always the valid argument that such shoots, if carefully taken off, will make cuttings for rooting after they have served their purpose as part of the floral decoration.

Irenes as cut-flowers   *Photo H. Bagust*

Geraniums are being used more for the decoration of public halls and have also been carried by bridesmaids at weddings. In most cases they have been included in bouquets, but they have also been used in little baskets. This surely is an idea which can, and I think will, be extended by many lovers of the geranium. The wide colour range and great variety of foliage available, will surely help to increase the cultivation of such remarkable and adaptable plants.

It is not easy for us to imagine a time when pelargoniums played an important role in the make-up of bouquets, posies and buttonholes. Today they are

The uses of Flowers and Foliage

not often used for these purposes, which is a great pity, since there are now so many remarkable varieties in all shapes and colours, and yet we still overlook them. It was at a time when the colour range was restricted that these flowers were so much in demand. The selection is now very wide, and the leaves themselves are often as attractively coloured as many flowers and these too, can be used for the make-up of buttonholes, bouquets, corsages and other designs.

The leaves usually need reinforcing so that they not only keep their shape but when placed behind the blooms, give a firm protection to the flower petals. It is best to use the 30-gauge wire and to lay a piece of this along the mid-rib of the leaf. Near the tip, make a small stitch, and then bring the end of the wire

Deacon Bonanza   *Photo H. Bagust*

back to the underside of the leaf again. The remainder of the wire should be brought down to the short leaf stem and twisted round it once or twice, until the base of the stem is reached.

When leaves are to be mounted in a bouquet or used as a part of a composite stem, much of the leaf stem should be removed. It is best to mount and wire each flower individually and this can be easily done by holding the flower downwards between the finger and thumb. Then pass a 30-gauge wire through one side to the other of the green calyx, leaving roughly equal portions on each side.

Practice will make it easy to fix wires where required, in order to keep both flowers and leaves in position. The wires can be covered with florist's tape, beginning quite near the base of the flower for extra strength. When using several different kinds of pelargoniums in a buttonhole or bouquet, it is best to place the darkest colour at the lowest point.

It is by no means essential to use the larger pelargoniums for this type of buttonhole or bouquet, since the nosegay type and fancy varieties are first class, many having frilled, almost double, flowers. The Regal pelargoniums certainly include these forms and many of them, by reason of their plush appearance, give a most pleasing effect. Geraniums and pelargoniums can also be used in modern flower arrangements, both flowers and foliage finding an increasing demand among enthusiasts.

It is a pity that most of the single flowered types shed their petals rather freely, although this can be largely overcome by the use of floral gum which although a somewhat tedious process, does allow the flowers to be used. The double and semi-double zonal varieties are first class in flower arrangements and if cut when half open and placed in water immediately, will last a long time and are less likely to become bruised when being handled.

The double flowers are of course, inclined to be a little heavier but if they are used with an abundance of unopened buds, this will lighten the effect.

Notes on the Judging of Pelargoniums

As a guide to exhibitors of pelargoniums the British Pelargonium and Geranium Society have prepared the folloing notes which are quoted by the permission of the Society.

Some of these are of a general character and others of specific application to particular types, having been compiled so that exhibitors will understand the standards against which entries at the Society's Annual Show and Competition will be judged.

GENERAL (applicable to all types)

Plants should be of good shape, proportionate in size to the size of the pot and foliated from the base, without blank spaces between plant and pot rim. Leaves should be clean, without evidence of insect injury or disease, of good colour with clear markings according to variety and neither coarse nor yellowing, in short, as visibly healthy as possible. Distorted or aged leaves should be removed. Flower heads should be held well clear of the foliage, proportionate in number to the size of the plant and of a bright, clear and distinct colour. Spent flowers should be removed. Pots should be clean.

SPECIFIC

28 (a) Groups or collections—Schedule conditions should be carefully studied

to ensure conformity both as to quantity and quality. Better effects are achieved when plants are culturally uniform.

(b) Zonals and regals–Flower heads should be of a minimum diameter of 2 in. or 5 centimetres and should not be too small or thin or have too few fully open flowers. A plant of five or more breaks should show three or more good flower heads and buds. In the case of the variegated leaved zonals, the retention of the flower heads or buds can be of importance in assessing the performance of the plant. Careful attention to the schedule conditions is important.

(c) Ivy-leaved and hybrid ivy-leaved–These may be grown with upright support or round frame or as a natural trailing plant. They should be shown in a floriforous state, the normal plant habit being to bloom in flushes.

(d) Scented leaved–The strength of scent, normal to the variety, is of prime importance, as is the colour and condition of the plant.

(e) Miniatures are deemed to be *mature plants normally less than 5 in. or 13 centimetres in height from soil level to the top of the foliage. The flower head should be carried clear of the foliage on a stem measuring not more than 5 in. or 13 centimetres from the junction with the main stem to the top of the flower head. Flowers may be single or double. Individual pips may be of any size and form. Leaves may be of any colour or colours but should not exceed 3½ in. or 9 centimetres across.

(f) Dwarfs are deemed to be *mature plants normally more than 5 in. or 13 centimetres but less than 8 in. or 20 centimetres in height from soil level to the top of the foliage. The flower head should be carried clear of the foliage on a stem measuring not more than 8 in. or 20 centimetres from the junction with the main stem to the top of the flower head. Flowers may be single or double. Individual pips may be of any size. Leaves may be of any colour or colours, not limited in size except that they must be proportionate to the size of the plant.

(g) Standards–A full standard should be 28 in. or 71 centimetres to the first break, a half standard 20 in. or 51 centimetres. Plants should be well furnished with flowers and buds.

(h) Floral arrangements–These classes will be judged in accordance with N.A.F.A.S. standards.

*A mature plant is one that has been cultivated under reasonably normal conditions for twelve months.

Plants and cut blooms should be clearly named. If the name of a plant is not known, it should be labelled 'name unknown'.

Seedlings should be labelled as such and the suggested name indicated. A seedling number may be shown instead of a name if this is preferred. Sports should be labelled as such. It should be borne in mind, that in accordance with International Nomenclature procedure, the name of a sport should include or bear specific reference to the name of the parent, e.g. Pink Happy Thought. At the first showing of a seedling, sport or new cultivar, full and relevant data should be provided, including parentage, name of raiser, date of raising and name of the person or nursery introducing it to commerce.

The table which follows indicates the allocation of a total of 20 points (25 for groups or collections) according to the qualities to be judged and exhibitors should note that is not constant for all types.

Hanging Basket   *Photo H. Smith*

STYLE

Type	Plant quality	Flower head	Pip	Colour	Foliage
Zonals (S., S.D., D.)					
Zonals cactus flowered					
Zonals rosebud	5	5	3	4	3
Zonals miniature and dwarf (other than variegated)					
Zonals coloured leaved					
Zonals miniature and dwarf (variegated)	8	2	2	2	6
Regals	5	4	3	5	3
Ivy and hybrid ivy-leaved					
green leaf	8	3	4	2	3
variegated leaf	6	2	–	4	8
Scented leaved	6	6 (scent)	2	2	4
Species, uniques and angels	8	4	2	2	4

30

The uses of Flowers and Foliage

Groups or collections	Plant quality 8	Varieties 4	Flower 4	Foliage 4	Display 5

	Colour	Quality	Form	Display
Cut blooms	4	6	6	4

DEFINITIONS

Pip = an individual flower (previously known as a floret)

Flower head = a cluster of pips growing from one stem (previously known as a truss)

Culture = length of stalk, shape of pip, absence of insect injury and disease

Form = size and shape of flower head, length of pins and number of pips

Pins = small stems holding pips to flower stalk.

Pot and paving   *Photo H. Smith*

In the days when sweet bags were much valued, the geranium leaves were largely used and among the recipes for these bags and cushions which were used 'to smell into for melancholy or to cause one to sleep', were dried rose leaves, scented geranium leaves, powdered mint and cloves. An old volume states that 'if these are put together in a bag and taken to bed with you, they will induce slumber'.

Also in some ancient books, there are indications that leaves of geraniums were used as healing agents especially in wounds made by any kind of metal or iron. Whether there is any scientific support for such assertions I am unable to say, but certainly many years ago, it was found that the leaves had some soothing value. In addition, it was believed that if an infusion of the leaves was made, and the resultant liquid dabbed into wounds, healing soon began.

Even the wild *Geranium robertianum*, is said to have been useful as a means of stopping internal bleeding and as an astringent to be used in connection with kidney troubles. Then there is the well-known Geranoil, an oil which is extracted from the foliage of the Rose geranium and which is still regarded as a marketable commodity in the South of France from where it is exported. In warm climates, the plants make bushy specimens almost four feet high.

Geranium capitatum or the Rose geranium, has leaves covered with soft hairs and a scent which is both spicy and rose-like. These leaves are sometimes used in cooking since they impart a rose-like flavour to custard puddings and jellies which, thus flavoured, were once considered a great delicacy. From the same leaves, a preserve can be made; this is known as geranium jelly. It was also once quite a custom to use the leaves of geraniums for flavouring jellies and custard. Both gooseberry and apple jellies assume a really lovely taste when flavoured in this way.

The foliage of the Rose geranium can also be employed to make a pretty garnish for sweet dishes, causing interest and pleasure. A further use for the same type of leaves is in perfuming caster sugar for sprinkling on cakes and other confectionery. The leaves are put into a stoppered jar of sugar and left there for a few days, their presence permeating the sugar so that when it is used, it will have a pleasing taste.

Years ago when the leaves were used for this purpose, it was widely believed that the geranium flavour imparted to the sugar, produced relief from various stomach discomforts. If the leaves are soaked for some hours in slightly warmed water and then kept in a corked bottle, the liquid can be used in the same way as eau de Cologne.

During recent years there have been references to geranium cakes. For these, the method is to lay six or seven leaves of the scented oak-leaved geranium at the bottom of the cake tin before an ordinary sponge mixture is poured in. When the cake is cooked, the leaves can be removed, by which time the delicate geranium flavour will be imparted to the whole cake.

Another use for geranium leaves is in the making of pot-pourri, although of course, rose petals, violet, jasmine and lavender flowers as well as sweet herbs, including bay leaves, should be included, but the real base of the mixture is the scented geranium leaves which provide the essential long-lasting scent.

The flowers and leaves must first be dried. A simple way of doing this is to spread them out on sheets of paper in an airy room, in dull light or they can be laid on flat trays in an airing cupboard which is not too hot. The once much-used silk bags or ornamental envelopes, had the scented geranium foliage included in their make-up, while dried and ground geranium leaves were added to the mixture when snuff was fashionable.

Geranium Punch has been tried and enjoyed in the United States, and some years ago a recipe for this drink appeared in the bulletin of the International Geranium Society. This was as follows. Pour one quart of boiling water over one pint of Rose geranium leaves. Let it stand for one hour, and then add one gallon of extra strong tea and some thin slices of lemon, with one cup of sugar. Put some leaves of the Rose geranium in each cube of a freezer tray, to add to each cup of punch. If desired, one quart of carbonated water may be added for effervescence.

Rose geranium rolls have also been made and used in the United States. To produce them, rolls should be prepared in the ordinary way. Then cube sugar should be marinated in grated orange rind and chopped Rose geranium leaves for several hours. Take a small piece of dough, flatten it out thinly and place a cube of sugar in the centre, pinching the dough up around the sugar. Let this rise until light, and bake in a quick oven.

Lastly, I like this extract from an 1846 diary, which was given in the Geranium Society's bulletin some years ago: 'Father always insisted that the lily could not be gilded, but when I became twenty, I was allowed to hide the pallor of my lips by rubbing the colour from red geraniums into them'. Having no need to use geranium petals in this way, I cannot vouch for the effectiveness of this suggestion.

Various Dwarf Geraniums in a greenhouse   *Photo F. G. Read*

3 Cultural requirements

SINCE THERE are no two growers who have exactly the same conditions for growing pelargoniums, it is impossible to give precise details for culture, since so much does depend on individual circumstances. The plants have, however, certain requirements which are needed for real success. This applies whether few plants are being grown by the amateur or many plants are being cultivated by the experienced professional grower.

It has often been said that geraniums grow best in poor soil, otherwise they will produce all foliage and no flowers. Again it has frequently been asserted that the plants should be kept fairly dry at the roots. Neither of these statements is correct, in fact. Although the plants *will* grow in impoverished soil, to do really well they must have a rooting medium in which there is plenty of goodness. It will just not do to use any old garden soil for growing plants in pots. For potting up at any time of the year, the John Innes Potting Composts are invaluable. These are standardized and generally available in three grades and do not require anything extra added, since they are so composed as to provide sufficient nourishment until the plants are potted up into large receptacles. The make-up of this compost is as follows: John Innes Potting Compost

No. 1, seven parts clean fibrous loam, three parts peat, two parts coarse silver sand and to each bushel of the mixture is added $\frac{3}{4}$ oz. of chalk and a $\frac{1}{4}$ lb. of base fertilizer. The latter consists of two parts hoof and horn meal, two parts superphosphate and one part potash, all by weight. The J.I. Potting Compost No. 2 has a double portion of base fertilizer and the No. 3 a treble portion.

These composts have proved to be quite sufficient to produce good plants, although if it is decided to use additional fertilizer as growth proceeds, avoid using those which are likely to cause rapid growth, which really means those which have an analysis showing a high percentage of nitrogen.

Perhaps one may wonder why ordinary garden soil is not recommended for potting purposes. It can be used of course, but a good potting mixture (not fancy mixtures containing artificials of unknown quantity or quality, which so often lead to forced growth, and the breakdown of the plant tissues) contains organic matter which holds moisture better than garden soil. These good composts are so made up as to be open and porous, promoting proper aeration and drainage. Although the John Innes composts are good, it must not be assumed that they are indispensable, for an ideal mixture can be made up with sweet loam, peat or leaf mould, silver sand, bone meal, and decayed sifted manure.

The modern theory that diseases must be expected is unsound, and I firmly believe that the frequency of their appearance nowadays, in almost any plant one cares to mention, is to a large extent because of wrong feeding, and the use of so many chemicals and chemico-biological treatments, applied on the flimsiest of pretexts, and also to a very large degree, by malnutrition or partial starvation, which has its beginning in wrong feeding. It is a mistaken idea that to cure disease, some kind of poisonous spray must be applied. Poison can never bring good health. The real answer to disease is to begin with healthy stock, and to grow it under hygienic conditions and provide proper nourishment.

Much has been heard during the past few years about foliar feeding. This of course, is simply the feeding of the plants through their leaves. A lot still remains to be discovered about this matter but undoubtedly many important trace elements can be absorbed in this way.

Tests show that the solution applied gains entry to the leaves, chiefly through the stomata or breathing pores. With some subjects these stomata are found on both sides, which is why care should be taken to spray on the undersides of the leaves. There is no doubt that leaf spraying does help to remedy certain conditions. For example, if there is iron chlorosis or boron deficiency because of heavy liming, foliar feeding is probably the best means of controlling the trouble.

Some deficiency diseases are worse in dry weather and it is often advisable to supplement the ordinary manuring programme with a foliar feed of trace elements if and when a spell of dry weather occurs.

There are various organic liquid fertilizers which benefit geraniums, including seaweed, of which there are now a number of proprietary brands. These can be be made up as directed and sprayed on to the foliage. Soot water has also given good results.

Foliar feeding can never take the place of the normal feeding through the roots but it can often remedy shortages of vital plant feeding materials in a little time.

Having made sure that the right soil conditions are provided, the plants have several other small, but important requirements, if real success is to be achieved. Fortunately, these do not include the provision of a large greenhouse, or any expensive-to-run routine, to ensure success. The plants will thrive even in the smallest type of glass structure, provided that in addition to their proper soil requirements being met, they have light, air, which includes ventilation, the right temperature and moisture as required. We will consider them in that order.

It is elementary to say that without light the leaves of the plants become yellow. This is an indication of the absence of chlorophyll, the substance of the green cells of the leaves. All of us have seen plants which have been kept in the dark for some time, with the result that the leaves have yellowed and eventually become colourless. This is particularly so when there is heat as well, since then, not only does growth become soft and pale, but the whole plant is weakened, with few if any flowers being produced. Geraniums cannot be grown well in deep shade outdoors or in a dark corner in the greenhouse.

With the many types of greenhouses now available, the accent has been to ensure all possible light reaching the plants being grown, and many houses are glazed to the ground. On the other hand, it is sometimes necessary to give some kind of shading during mid-summer. Not a lot is needed; in fact, just sufficient to prevent the rays of the sun from falling directly on to the plants. The pelargonium, being of South African origin, likes sun of course, but glass is inclined to bring about leaf scorch and other troubles, as well as drying out the compost quickly. This causes the blooms to become bleached and the leaves to lose their liveliness. Where blinds are fitted to the house they are ideal for shading, since they can be used as required. Strips of hessian or even paper can be fixed up just to keep off the direct rays of the sun. Failing this, whiting or Summer Cloud can be painted on to the glass, although with these, there is the bother of washing them off later.

The question of temperature is an important one as far as the pelargonium is concerned, and can be largely controlled by ventilation, for by this means it is possible to ensure that the plants do not become weak and drawn and therefore susceptible to disease.

Most glasshouses are well fitted with ventilators, but even so, common sense is necessary in their use, for when opened, they not only let out the hot air but also admit more fresh air, so that they must be used in such a way as to avoid draughts, being opened before the heat becomes very great and closed to prevent very low night temperatures. Regularity in giving ventilation is a necessity. As far as possible a temperature between 55 and 65 degrees Fahrenheit should be considered the ideal, although in summer, it will probably rise at periods, to considerably more. This is the time that proper ventilation is essential. During the coldest months it may not be possible to raise the temperature to more than 50 degrees, with an even lower drop at night, but definite steps should be made to ensure that it does not fall below 45 degrees, particularly if one is aiming at having winter or very early spring flowers.

Experience has proved that although pelargoniums will stand fluctuations in temperature, they will not do well in continuous great heat. For keeping the plants in healthy condition with foliage of good colour, a very dry atmosphere should be avoided, so that in general an occasional damping of the greenhouse floor and staging should be given to provide the humid conditions necessary for good results.

What about moisture requirements? This is a question which demands attention, for even if soil make-up, temperature and ventilation are right, if the plants' roots are kept either too dry or too wet, trouble is bound to occur. Pelargoniums will certainly stand hard treatment but require good conditions if they are to give a first-class display. They will not survive without moisture, which is being absorbed by the roots all the time. Having provided good drainage for the receptacles in which the plants are growing, it is only natural that the water applied will be used fairly quickly and will need regular replacement. Even in winter, a little moisture will be required at times by established plants, for the belief that no water is needed by pelargoniums during the shortest days, is a fallacy. During the growing season it is best to water thoroughly when required and then not to water again until the soil is almost dry. Avoid giving daily sprinklings.

Pelargoniums are not hardy and frost will destroy them, although so long as the foliage and stems are dry, they will stand low temperatures fairly well. If the leaves are damp or the roots are in soggy soil, the plants will soon be injured. This is one reason why the plants require so little watering during the winter. There are records of zonal varieties standing several degrees of frost without harm.

In avoiding damp conditions during the winter, care must be taken not to go to the other extreme. The practice sometimes advised, of knocking the plants out of pots and tying the roots in bundles, and then hanging them up in the greenhouse or shed during the winter, is nothing short of folly. The fact that occasionally, some plants have survived despite this bad treatment, is a further indication of how good tempered is the geranium.

As to the means of heating the greenhouse, or other glass structure being used, there are several good ways of doing this, and although hot water pipes still provide the ideal way of giving the warmth needed, there are now many easy-to-work-and-regulate electric heaters, which are inexpensive to use. Of these, there are some which can be thermostatically controlled, and once set, the thermostat maintains the required temperature. Gas heating too, is sometimes employed, but in this connection, it is essential that no fumes enter the house, otherwise the plants are bound to suffer. Where no other method is practicable, paraffin oil lamps can be used; while not ideal, there are many instances of complete success being achieved by this means, although here again, no fumes should be allowed to escape among the plants. This is often a difficulty, but provided the oil stove is kept clean, regularly trimmed and not handled carelessly, so as to spill the oil, such stoves can be quite efficient. In this connection, the Eltex oil burning greenhouse heater can be recommended with confidence. It is rigidly constructed in galvanized sheet steel, has easily removable lamps which can be filled without difficulty and a detachable moisture tray that helps to provide an atmosphere which does not become too dry or fume laden.

A point to remember in regard to the use of paraffin burners, is that they are not capable of being controlled automatically and the ordinary blue flame burner has no latitude of adjustment. Therefore, once lit these heaters go on burning regardless of the varying requirements of the greenhouse, until either they run out of paraffin or are intentionally extinguished. However,

37

they are reasonably cheap to run when they are used intermittently. That is, if they are lighted up when artificial heat is essential, and if they are put out again as soon as they are not required.

The question of fumes is a most important one. Products of the perfect combustion of paraffin, including carbon dioxide, are not harmful to growing plants. Dangerous fumes are given off only if combustion is imperfect. In a good greenhouse, the heated metal of the chimney or other piping on the paraffin heaters, plays a vital part in ensuring perfect combustion and the absence of harmful fumes. Besides this, the actual make-up of these parts is an important factor in the effective distribution of heat.

The worst feature of imperfect combustion is its failure to convert the poisonous carbon monoxide. It is, of course, free carbon monoxide which kills plants, and is certainly harmful to human beings too. There are several causes why this is given off, even when the best type of heater is used. They include an improperly adjusted or carbonized wick, lack of proper ventilation and poor quality, impure paraffin.

There should certainly be no trouble if the wick is trimmed regularly and the burner is kept perfectly clean and free from carbon deposits and spilt paraffin, with of course, proper adjustment. A watch should be kept for an appearance of any tongues of yellow flame which if seen, indicate that particles of carbon are on the wick and need removing. It is always advisable to use good quality paraffin, for the lower grades often contain a number of impurities including sulphur, in excess of the safe minimum. It is this excessive sulphur which sometimes combines with hydrogen, causing the terrible smell often connected with paraffin oil burners.

The purest grades of paraffin are now coloured blue, green or pink, and it is really best to depend upon one of these grades for greenhouse heating. Although paraffin is sometimes treated with salt or camphor, this is certainly not necessary or even desirable, if good quality liquid is used.

It must be made clear that fumes should not be confused with the smell or odour of paraffin, since they are quite distinct. It is because carbon monoxide is entirely without smell, and its presence cannot be detected in this way, that it is so harmful to plants. It is possible for growing plants to be damaged or spoiled before it is realized that fumes are escaping. A really good heater kept in a house which is adequately ventilated, will not give off harmful fumes. It is too much to expect that the well-known smell of paraffin will never be noticed, but this will not damage plants. In fact, a heater which gives out a normal paraffin smell might be doing its job much better than one from which there is no smell at all, but which might possibly be emitting the harmful poisonous fumes.

Pollination   *Photo F. G. Read*

4 Propagation

Securing Seed

Among the methods of propagation which are open to both the professional
and amateur geranium grower is that of raising plants from seed. It does
however, demand much patience for it is quite a long process and in any
case, only a small proportion, if any, of the seedlings raised will come true to
the type of plant from which the seed was collected. Against this, there is the
interest of awaiting results and the possibility (even although extremely slight)
of raising a plant with some distinct qualities and one which will be worth
perpetuating.

Several specialist growers now offer hand-pollinated seed, in some instances
giving the names of the parents from which the seed has come. In some cases,
crosses have been made by combining likely parents to produce compact
growth, particular shades of coloured plants, with free flowering capabilities.
There is however no reliable 'key' by which to work.

39

On the other hand, seed pods can be picked from plants of which the flowers have been pollinated through the activity of bees and other insects or by the winds or rains. The geranium is not a flower which is self-pollinating like, for example, the Sweet Pea. It is one of a group of plants which are said to have protandorous flowers, that is the stamens first develop and the little pollen sacs ripen and burst before the stigma or female part of the flowers develop. This naturally means that unless bees or some other agent cause pollen to be deposited on the stigma when it has developed and is in a receptive condition, seed cannot form. This makes hand pollination a simple task, especially since the need for emasculation does not exist.

Even so, when pollen from the finest varieties is used, it does not by any means follow that any of the seedlings raised will make worthwhile new plants. In very many cases, the seedlings revert and become similar to a primitive ancestor and at other times, the flowers which develop are so near to one of the parents that the plants could not be given a name. Other seedlings will be found to be of poor constitution or have other undesirable characteristics, so that it must be said that the possibility of securing a really tip-top new variety is very remote.

However, it is the persistence of the plant grower that makes him what he is–always an optimist–and since there is always a chance, slight though it may be, that something good will be produced, no real enthusiast will be undaunted when it comes to seeing what he can grow in the way of seedlings. To save cluttering up one's greenhouse with seedlings of little merit, it is necessary to be absolutely ruthless in cutting out everything not of the very highest standard.

What then is the process by which seeds are obtained? Having selected the parents, remembering that the flower of the female parent should be a day or two in advance of the male parent, it is wise to carefully cover the former with a paper or similar thin bag, to ensure that no insect or other agent transfers pollen to the receptive stigma. Before this is done, some of the buds from the truss of the female parent should be removed, leaving eight to ten buds of about the same size, so that all open about the same time.

Some growers have found it an advantage to withhold water from plants just at the fertilizing stage, for it seems that very frequently, a much better set of seed results under fairly dry root conditions. The selected male parent should be watched so that when the little sacs on the top of the stamens, commonly known as anthers, are ripe, and burst releasing the pollen grains, the latter can be used on the flower selected for the female parent.

When the pollen is ready, the protective covering is taken from the female flower and the actual pollinating should then be carried out with great care. Mid-morning, or at any rate before noon, seems to be the best time of day for the job which is most simple. It only requires the use of a very clean, fine camel hair brush to transfer most carefully, the pollen from the stamens on to the receptive stigma of the female parent. This will be slightly sticky, thus enabling the pollen to adhere easily.

Particularly with very special varieties, it is wise to re-cover the pollinated flower, the bag being removed when it is seen, normally within a few days, that a little seed pod is forming. Provided pollination has been effective (for of course, pollinated blooms do not necessarily become fertilized, although most do), and as soon as the petals fall, the long pointed seed vessel will quickly take on the shape of a Stork's-bill which as already explained, is why the geranium is sometimes given this name.

Given plenty of light the seed pod will soon ripen when the seed can be harvested in the usual way and later, may be sown in an attempt to raise something really new and worthwhile. Seed harvested when unripe, will prove useless. Even when two parents most likely to produce something very startling are crossed, it is by no means certain that any seedlings of real value will materialize.

Frequent examination of the pods is necessary to prevent the seed being lost when the pod splits unnoticed, since the hairspring-like tail on the end unfolds rapidly, causing the seed to be ejected and fall to the ground, often some little distance from the actual plant.

Therefore, when particular crosses have been made, it is wisest to gather the seed pods just before they are quite ripe and place them in a box or other receptacle. At the first signs of the pod splitting, the seeds can be shaken out into a bag and will be ready for sowing as required, which for best results, should be within a month of gathering.

As to the sowing, the little tail should first be cut from each seed, most of which will germinate freely, so long as it is fresh when sown, usually within twelve to fifteen days. In some cases, a very much longer time elapses, so that it is unwise to disturb the compost too soon. It is of course, necessary to remove seedlings as they become ready for potting up.

No elaborate seed sowing mixture is required and the John Innes seed compost is very suitable, although a simple mixture can easily be made by using any good sifted loam, peat, and silver sand plus, where possible, some well-decayed manure.

Artificial fertilizers are best entirely avoided, for they tend to induce rapid top growth, without a corresponding root system. Water must be applied as necessary, but if the compost is made and kept too sodden, the seed may rot. Seed pans or boxes can be used and the seed covered with an eighth of an inch of compost. They should be kept in an even temperature, around 55 to 60 deg. F. (13 to 16 deg. C.) and when big enough to handle, the seedlings must be transferred to small pots and then to larger ones as growth proceeds. The period between seed sowing and the seedlings flowering must be one of patience, since it generally means waiting well over a year and sometimes up to eighteen months, before the value of the flowering capabilities of the young plants can be assessed. Sometimes, although a young plant may show evidence of being of merit, it may have other traits which offset its good qualities, so that it will be for the grower to decide whether to retain it. It may be possible to outbreed by further selection, any undesirable points and replace them with those which will ensure a plant of real value. It is not worth wasting time on inferior plants but rather to set a high standard and stick to it, otherwise a lot of space will be taken up by second-rate plants.

Regarding the naming of seedlings the International Congress on Nomenclature recommends that personal names should no longer be given to new varieties. The hybridist should not attempt to perpetuate his name or that of a friend by giving it to a new plant he has created.

Cuttings

Although comparatively few geranium growers go in for raising plants from   41 seed, a very large quantity of plants are propagated from cuttings. This is not to be wondered at, for as already indicated, by the seed method, several months must elapse before a flowering size plant is secured. From cuttings, a really good, well-rooted plant can be had in about two months.

Furthermore, one can be sure that by propagating by cuttings the new plants secured will be identical in every way to the plants from which the cuttings were taken. This is most important when perpetuating a variety with special qualities. With large growing plants, the taking of cuttings will do more than provide a good stock of young plants for it will, if the cuttings are carefully removed, keep the parent plants of good shape and prevent the development of elongated specimens with woody, crowded stems.

Theoretically the best plants are obtained from the tops or growing points of the stems, for normally the strongest, liveliest activity is there. The length of the cuttings should be 3 or 4 inches with about three joints. It is hardly necessary to say that cuttings should not be taken from plants which do not flower or those which appear to have some undesirable characteristics.

There is perhaps no actual close season for taking cuttings but undoubtedly the majority are secured in August and September, usually when stock plants are being prepared for their winter quarters, in many cases being brought in from outdoor beds. Cuttings taken in the autumn will need slight heat during the winter and by the following May and June, will normally prove to be fully capable of producing a good supply of bloom throughout the whole of the summer.

February and March are other good months too, for securing cuttings and under ordinary cultivation these will become well rooted in about three weeks after being inserted. Often, these cuttings will prove to be as satisfactory in the way of early blooms as autumn struck cuttings.

Whilst cuttings can be made in every other month, it is really best to avoid November and December, since then they are more likely to damp off with Black Rot of the stem. As to the actual selecting and preparing of the cuttings, it is best not to use excessively soft and sappy growth. These are often produced on plants which are not very free flowering, in seasons where there has not been much sun to ripen the stems.

The lower leaves and stipules should be removed, but at least two leaves should be left. Failure to do this will result in delayed rooting and the risk of damping off.

The old-fashioned practice of leaving the cuttings out of the soil for a few hours after they have been taken is not a sound one, although it was very frequently done on one of the nurseries at which I received my training. It is best to have the compost ready so that the cuttings can be inserted as soon as they are taken. It is generally supposed that this exposing treatment will cause the freshly severed bottom end of the cutting to become rapidly sealed by the formation of a layer of 'skin', but the desirable sealing does of course, form naturally when the cuttings have been inserted in the compost. The only exception to this is when it is necessary to propagate from very soft cuttings, since then it does seem probable that there is some value in allowing the cut ends to dry by being exposed to the cool air for some time.

It is essential for good results to make a perfectly clean cut immediately below the node or joint and this means a really sharp knife is indispensable, for a torn or jagged base will invite the entry of disease as will the making of

The potting bench　　　　　　　　　　　　　*Photo F. G. Read*

a cut in between the joints. It is at the joints that the cell activity is the greatest and where the leaves form most readily.

Incidentally, one of the advantages of using a rooting compost containing sand or of inserting the cuttings in pure sand, as is sometimes advised, is that the sand touching the base of the cuttings stimulates them, causing the root 'points' to form very quickly after callousing has occurred. With large quantities of cuttings and where there is the convenience available, the cuttings can be rooted in clean sand or very sandy compost in a frame from which it is possible to exclude frost and maintain a temperature of 55 to 60 deg. F. (13 to 16 C.). Watering must be done with care, in fact, after an initial good watering to settle the soil firmly around the cuttings, they should be kept rather on the dry side.

Seed boxes too, may be used for the cuttings but the best method is to use the small, so-called thumb pots, for they not only save soil, but since the roots work freely into the little pots, when potting on is necessary, there is not the slightest check in growth and the possibility of Black Leg is minimized. The plunging of the pots into a bed of peat is a great aid to growth, especially where there is the provision of soil warming through the use of electric wires.

For the small grower, and where space is limited, the best way of growing on the cuttings is either to insert them singly in small pots or put a number round the edge of a 5-inch pot. The first potting is done in the 60 or 2½-inch

43

diameter size pots in which, in the case of autumn rooted cuttings, the young plants are kept during the winter.

The ideal way of keeping young stock during the winter is to plunge the pots into sandy soil or peat, in a frost-proof frame, but since such a facility is not available to the average gardener, it means keeping the plants in the greenhouse or living-room. There, the temperature should centre around 55 to 60 deg. F. (13 to 16 C.) and should never fall below 40 deg. F. (6 C.). Plenty of light, little water and a rather dry atmosphere should be the aim.

In the early spring, it is necessary to pinch out the growing points of the cuttings, so as to induce the formation of bushy plants. Do not take too much off, for not only will this tend to delay the proper development of side shoots, but it makes the entry of disease easier. As the plants begin to produce flower buds in the spring, a little feeding can be started, but it is again stressed that nitrogenous fertilizers should be applied sparingly.

Success with cuttings comes when they are potted firmly and about an inch or an inch and a half deep, without the soil being rammed around them. When the soil is made very firm, proper drainage and porosity are prevented. This does not mean that the cuttings should be left loose or insecure. Plenty of light should be given and a good place for the young plants, especially very early spring secured cuttings, is on the shelves or staging near the glass. Dead leaves should be carefully removed so as to minimize the possible entry of disease, while frequent syringings of clear water will be beneficial.

An American floriculturist has this to say about geranium propagation, in *Florists Exchange*:

'Geraniums are the most important spring bedding plant and as such deserve more attention than they usually receive'.

'Too frequently their production is fitted into the growing schedule without much thought given to the needs of the crop. They need a soil with good physical condition; 25 per cent by volume of peat moss helps. Keep the soluble salts low. Soil from old bench crops are frequently high in soluble salts. Geraniums do well in light soil with a medium nutrient level.

'Follow a regular spray schedule. Stock plants should be well protected, particularly immediately after cuttings are taken. Stock plants in benches can be watered by the injection system. Plants watered from underneath can be kept in good production for four or more years. The dry soil surface which results from injection watering, greatly reduces the disease problem.

'Place the cuttings in a clean rooting medium only. The Blackleg problem often seems to start near the edges of wooden benches. Cleaning up the propagating bench between plantings helps a great deal. If cuttings are placed in $2\frac{1}{4}$- or $2\frac{1}{2}$-inch pots, use new or sterilized pots'.

It must not be thought that all new varieties are the result of cross-fertilization or hybridizing, for there have been many cases of sports or mutations in pelargoniums and in fact they are always likely to appear and frequently do, although only the most obvious ones are noticed. Sometimes they are definitely worth saving and propagating in order to work up a stock. If as the result of such treatment, the sport remains true in every way, does not revert and has qualities which make it desirable, stock can be increased vegetatively as necessary.

Propagation

It seems certain that the first double zonal raised in France over ninety years ago, first appeared as a sport. This happening was certainly a great event in the history of the geranium, for it was the appearance of this first double that has enabled hybridists to produce many of the double and semi-double varieties which are in cultivation today.

It was of course, necessary for the first double to be recognized as a definite break and this is why it is always wise to take notice of any sport, or in fact any plant raised from seed which is different, just in case they may be further breaks of value.

There are still several colours which are desirable in zonal geraniums and we all look for the coming of a real yellow and a pure blue. There are of course, blue-mauves, which are sometimes referred to as blue, but so far there is not any really true blue zonal. This, of course, is why the growing of pelargoniums is always interesting and sometimes rewarding.

The present widespread popularity of the pelargonium as a bedding and pot plant is fully deserved. Apart from the delightful show these plants give, both in regard to their flowers and very often their foliage too, they are among the best tempered plants in cultivation. They will withstand quite a lot of ill-treatment, and even neglect, but when given ordinary good care, they respond to a remarkable degree.

Although there are now in cultivation several hundred good varieties, many being of fairly recent introduction, quite a number of the older and more exotic-looking sorts have recently been brought back into cultivation. It must be said however, that some of the rare kinds are not quite so easy to manage as the more usual sorts since they have less stamina.

As we have seen, geraniums are easily propagated by cuttings; in fact, this is the best method by which to increase a stock quickly. As far as possible, cuttings should be secured from selected stock plants, which have been grown on specially for propagating purposes.

It never does to attempt to secure cuttings from 'any old plant' and even in cases where apparently good plants are bedded out, it is often somewhat difficult to select material which is entirely free from disease. A method which can be recommended is to bed out a number of stock plants in a frame, which should be kept open during the summer. The soil in the frame should be well drained, and have a high organic content.

Pelargoniums thrive where there is an abundance of water, but excesses must be avoided at all costs, or soft cuttings with long internodes, difficult to root, will be produced. For the same reason, fertilizers with a high phosphorus and potassium content should be used, whilst nitrogen should be supplied only in comparatively small quantities.

Cuttings can be taken practically throughout the entire growing season, and where flowering plants are required during the winter, it is a good plan to take a batch of cuttings in March, and April, so that these develop well throughout the summer. Such specimens should be stopped occasionally, to promote bushy growth, and when the flower buds appear, they should be picked off until late September, when the plants are taken into the greenhouse and kept in a temperature of around 55 degrees F. Such plants should give a bright display of flowers during the winter months.

Undoubtedly, the best plants are obtained for general purposes, from cuttings rooted during the months of July, August and September. The first batch can be secured or 'sneaked' as some growers say, while the plants are still in their summer flowering positions.

The aim should be to secure cuttings between 3 and 4 inches long, although they may be taken shorter at times, when stock is scarce. Such specimens should have fairly firm stems, with two or three joints. Only the bottom leaves are removed, and at least two perfect leaves are kept on each cutting. Failure to do this may result in delayed rooting, with an increased risk of damping off. The cuts should be made with a sharp clean knife, and the lower leaves and stiples carefully removed. Any flower buds which are present should also be stripped off.

Some gardeners let the prepared cutting dry by exposure to air for some hours, and there is still some considerable difference of opinion among experts as to whether this is a wise action. Personally, I think it is better to pot up the cuttings immediately they are taken, placing several around the rim of a pot, or they can be put in singly, if small pots are used.

A properly made cut inserted in a suitable soil mixture should lead to the quick production of roots. The speed, efficiency, and vigour of the root production, depends upon the activity of the hormones or growth relating substances, which occur naturally within the stem. These become most active at the points, which is why the cut is made in that position. It is because the activity of the hormones is slower that some varieties of geraniums are rather shy in rooting, the lack of the natural supply of these growth relating hormones being inadequate. This is why growth substances have been prepared by manufacturing chemists for they augment the natural supply in the stems.

Whilst many gardeners are against the use of such preparations, it has been found that in certain instances at least they are a help in providing a greater uniformity of growth. These are available in both powder and liquid forms, they are quick and easy to use, and either the cutting base is soaked in the diluted liquid for twenty-four hours or so, or it is stirred in the powder, being gently tapped to remove any excess of powder. Should the stem be very dry, making it difficult for the powder to adhere, it can be moistened first by dipping it in clean water, although if this is done, care must be taken that too much powder does not stick to the cutting base. It is essential to carry out instructions for use, as given on the containers of the hormone powders and liquids.

The best method of rooting the cuttings is to use a good simple compost, made up of loam, peat and silver sand. This provides the right texture, for the compost should be open so that it drains freely without any suggestion at all of clogging. At the same time the compost should retain moisture, but it does not need to be rich. At this stage, and certainly until the plants are rooted nicely, they do not need feeding, for the aim should be to encourage the production of a good root system, and the amount of foliage is really immaterial. The John Innes Compost No. 1, is quite suitable, although by no means essential.

Where a large number of cuttings are being prepared, they can be inserted in shallow trays or boxes, or even on the greenhouse bench although there is really nothing better than the ordinary clay pots since they do make handling easy and there is no difficulty when the cuttings have to be potted up singly. So long as the compost is really open and drains well, it is not essential to crock the drainage holes of the pots, although this has long been the custom.

When inserting the cuttings they should be put firmly into the soil without however, making it really hard, for this would deter the roots from breaking out easily.

It is always unwise to use a pointed instrument for making the hole for the cutting, for then there is always the danger that a cavity may be left at the bottom and this would act as a water holder. Cuttings can also be rooted in the frame lights using either a good compost, or even clean silver sand. Immediately the cuttings have been inserted they should be given a good watering, after which they should be kept slightly on the dry side.

As a guide, about 200 cuttings will occupy a square yard of frame space, this allowing a suitable distance between each cutting. Whether the cuttings are started in the greenhouse or frame, the aim should be to provide a temperature of just over 50 degrees F. and in the event of sunshine, shade will have to be provided and draughts too should be guarded against. Great care is needed in regard to watering since it is only necessary to water when moisture is really needed. Then a thorough soaking should be given and water withheld until the compost is almost dry again.

Where a large number of cuttings are being taken from various stock plants, care is needed in order to prevent the spread of virus troubles and for this reason, it is a good plan to wipe the knife used for cuttings with some kind of disinfectant. It is all too easy to transfer virus from plant to plant by not being careful in this respect.

The length of time taken for cuttings to root depends on the time of year and the variety. In some cases, under good conditions, root development begins almost at once, although even then, such rooted cuttings will not be ready for potting on for at least three of four weeks. After that of course, the plants are moved to bigger pots according to the growth they make, although there is no need to do anything to hasten growth in the autumn.

Experience shows, that although the Black Vesuvius varieties are members of the zonal group, they respond best if the cuttings are taken from them during the first three months of the year. If they can be rooted on a bench where there is some bottom heat, this will be of great help. Whilst growth hormones have been found useful for these varieties, they do need rather more care in regard to watering and ventilation, since neglect in these respects may lead to leaf fall and other troubles.

Grafting

A much less usual way of propagating geraniums is by grafting. This is a first-class method of improving plants which make a small amount of growth and which never seem able to develop into really good sized free flowering plants. It is no use giving such plants heavy doses of manure or fertilizer, and the best way of improving them, in fact often the only way, is to graft them on to a vigorous variety. This can be done in April.

It is necessary to select vigorous plants to use as root stocks, and strong specimens having two or three well ripened, fairly thick branches should prove suitable. Ideally, a plant with three branches is best, since then two branches can be grafted and the remaining one left to grow and thereby draw up sap, by which the plant is kept alive, and to make use of the surplus sap which will be present after grafting.

Then the cuttings to be inserted must be selected, and these should roughly   **47** be of about the same thickness as the branches on the root stock. They should have one or two smallish leaves on them. In preparation for the operation, it is advisable to have on hand a sharp knife, a strip of half-inch wide polythene, some adhesive tape, a glass jar and a thin cane for each graft.

To begin the operation, shorten the branch which is to be grafted, making a slanting cut, preferably just below a leaf joint, afterwards shaving off the point of the slant so that the top of the branch is of the shape of an inverted letter V. Prepare the cutting to be inserted by making a V-shaped end, then cut downwards, not quite to the centre of the bottom, repeat the same on the opposite side. The branch on which the cut is to be inserted must also be split down the middle by placing a knife across the centre of the top, and pressing downward to the required depth. Gradually withdraw the knife until only the tip is invisible, then gently twist the knife which will cause the graft to open wider at the top. The graft must then be inserted, sliding it from the top as you push it down to the tip of the knife. The object must be to see that the rind or outer skin of both the plant and the graft are flush at the outside. Make sure that air does not enter, for this would dry up the wounds. Therefore, a strip of polythene should be applied as soon as possible just below the graft, and wound around both upwards and downwards in order to seal the graft. Over the polythene, a strip of adhesive tape can be applied, although this tape must not be allowed to adhere to the rind itself, or it will cause damage when it is taken off later.

Then place a thin cane into the soil in the pot so that it is just a couple of inches above the graft. It is advisable to cover grafted plants with a bell cloche, or even a large jam jar, making sure that this rests on the cane, and just covers the graft to the fork of the branch. The leaves should be free and not in contact with the glass. If they are, they will soon become discoloured and wilt, and this may very well prevent the graft from being successful.

Keep the grafted plants in a shady part of the greenhouse and as necessary, give an occasional or light spraying of water so that the atmosphere does not become too dry.

After five or six weeks, and if the plant remains firm and the leaves have not wilted too seriously, it may be assumed that the graft is successful. When the graft has made two inches of fresh growth, the bandage can be removed and the plant should gradually develop into a vigorous new specimen. It can then be grown on in the usual way.

Considerable interest has been shown in the propagation of geraniums by leaf or leaf axil cuttings. This method was defined by Mr. Leonard Harrison in publications of the British Geranium Society. They were based on his own experiments which showed successful results of between 50 and 70 per cent of the axil cuttings taken. Later, in the case of certain varieties, including 'Abel Carriere', good roots had formed within eighteen days, on 90 per cent of the cuttings taken.

The procedure is first to take cuttings in the usual way, these are two or three leaves longer than are needed for rooting. Instead of breaking off the spare leaves, cut about $\frac{1}{4}$-inch below the joint you are going to use. The other leaves will make axil cuttings. Cut the stem $\frac{1}{4}$ inch above and below the leaf, and then cut the stem lengthwise, leaving about a third on the leaf stalk. Pare the top and bottom to a wedge shape and the cutting is ready.

48 Use a rooting medium of two parts, by bulk, of sedge peat, and one part

sharp silver sand well mixed together and rubbed through a $\frac{3}{4}$-inch sieve. Then bury the stalk part of the cutting to a depth of about $\frac{1}{2}$ inch. For preference, keep the boxes on a heated bench or some other place where there is bottom heat, which is desirable for this method of propagation. Soak the cuttings well and afterwards give overhead sprayings of water at five- or six-hourly intervals. If the bottom heat can be retained at 65 deg. F. (19 C.) the air temperature is not quite so important and can in fact vary between 50 and 80 deg. F. (10–26 C.) without in any way retarding growth of the roots.

The best time for taking leaf cuttings is in the spring, although it can go on until mid-July. Before taking the cuttings it is essential to ensure that there is a bud in each leaf axil. This may be very tiny but unless one is there, it is a waste of time to insert the leaf cuttings.

Experiments have shown that the use of hormone rooting powder does not seem to have any advantage; in fact, the cuttings thus treated were actually longer in rooting. An interesting fact is that leaf cuttings make a larger cluster of fibrous roots than is produced by cuttings taken in the normal way, although the plants take longer to come into flower.

Sowing the seeds

Pelargoniums can be raised from seed, particularly where new forms are required as hybrids. Pelargonium species will, of course, breed true. As indicated earlier, there is something adventurous in sowing seeds of the hybrids, for they rarely breed true to the parent and variations occur in colour, leaf form, habit and general size of the plants.

Pelargonium (geranium) seeds are normally offered in mixtures and the resultant seedlings can be of great interest. Germination often occurs in a short period, on other occasions quite a long time elapses before there are signs of growth. If seed is being saved from plants already in one's possession the feathered tails should be cut off and for preference, the seed sown within a month or so after gathering, although seed will actually remain viable for several years if stored correctly.

A good ordinary seed-sowing mixture can be used, such as the John Innes type, or a mixture can be made up of equal parts of leaf mould, silver sand and loam, since nothing very rich is required. Use boxes or pans, which should be well crocked to ensure good drainage and then bring the soil mixture to within $\frac{1}{2}$ inch of the rim, lightly pressing and smoothing it down, but not making it too hard. Sow the seed thinly and evenly on the surface, pressing it down gently. Then cover with up to $\frac{1}{4}$ inch of finely sifted soil and finish off with a fine sprinkling of water.

If the receptacles are covered with a pane of glass and paper, this will keep the compost from drying out, especially if the containers are placed out of direct sunlight and are kept in a temperature of around 55 degrees F. After about a fornight, signs of growth should be seen, although cases have been known where many months have elapsed before germination was evident.

Although it has always been possible to raise mixed hybrid geraniums from seed, it is only recently that seed of separately coloured sorts have become available.

Nittany Lion was the first really good geranium to come true from seed. It produces strong compact plants bearing large flower heads of bright scarlet. In this country germination has been irregular and flowering erratic.

The Carefree strains which are F.1 hybrids have become widely known during the last few years and they are available separately in pink, salmon and scarlet. They can certainly be had in flower early in the green house, but out of doors they are often very late in producing flower buds.

An F.2 mixture known as Fleuriste, forms robust growing plants the colours including scarlet, salmon-pink, picotee and white. In the 1972 All Britain Trials, an F.1 hybrid named Sprinter was awarded a Bronze Medal. The bright scarlet flowers are earlier and the plants dwarfer than any other geranium grown from seed. L'Amour is the name of a new F.1 strain of dwarf geraniums easily raised from seed.

The period between seed sowing and the seedlings' flowers must be one of patience, since it means waiting six to nine months, sometimes much longer, before a flower of sufficient size is produced to enable one to value the possibilities of the new plant.

In the case of variegated varieties, the variegation does not show in the seed leaves and very often not in the first true leaves either. It is essential to be somewhat hard hearted in retaining seedlings, otherwise one can become cluttered up with inferior specimens which will never prove really worth growing.

The young plants must be potted on as necessary, but it is a mistake to provide pots which are too large, since a lot of soil in a pot without roots permeating the compost will soon become sour. Geraniums do not require extra rich fare, particularly in the young stages. They should be encouraged to build up sturdy stem growth rather than a lot of weak shoots.

A border of Dwarf Geraniums

5 Bedding out

SEVENTY YEARS ago, the geranium or zonal pelargonium ranked among the most popular of plants for use as summer bedding. They certainly fell from popularity for this purpose, but during the last thirty years or so, there has been greatly renewed interest in using them in many parts of the country.

In spite of the claims of rival bedding plants which have been introduced during recent years, geraniums can still hold their own against all comers. They are unbeatable when used as bedding subjects in smoky and dusty towns. Many park superintendents have reason to be satisfied with the toughness and tolerance of these plants, particularly in crowded city parks, where not only the atmosphere may be unfavourable but damage from children and dogs may be among the other hazards. Geraniums may be relied upon to give a good show whatever the season is like, although obviously, in a wet year, the display is not so good as during a sunny season.

There are of course, many varieties of geraniums which do well as pot plants, but prove quite unsuitable for bedding out in the open. The landscape gardener looks for varieties which have plenty of vigour and which do not grow straggly.

Sometimes a plant will throw up tall coarse shoots quite out of character with the rest of the plant. This is usually due to excessive nitrogenous manuring, or the uneven distribution of other types of fertilizers or manures. To be satisfactory, bedding geraniums must not only be able to stand up to wet weather but must be free-flowering and keep their colour well, even during spells of strong sunshine.

Freedom from or resistance to pests and diseases, are other desirable advantages. The petals should not fall off too readily, and in this connection, the double varieties certainly have a big advantage. The colour should also be held fast, for flowers that fade or discolour quickly through climatic conditions, are not really suitable for bedding. It is also desirable that the blooms should be carried erect and above the foliage.

It has often been noticed that winds which will even shatter the flowers of 'Paul Crampel', leave 'Gustav Emich' untouched. This is one reason why the latter is so largely used for bedding, and it is undoubtedly one of the most satisfactory geraniums for this purpose. For those who prefer a deeper shade of scarlet, there is 'Decorator'.

'King of Denmark' has long been used for bedding purposes, while 'Mrs. Lawrence' is more compact and if anything, even more free flowering. In the salmon shades, 'Queen of Denmark' and 'The Speaker' are good sorts, while as a double white for bedding, 'Hermine' is first class, and for a deep crimson, 'Royal Purple' is reliable. 'A. M. Mayne' is one of the few purple coloured varieties which can be recommended but to produce best results, it should be given ground on the poor side and be planted firmly in soil which does not remain constantly wet. Otherwise, it is liable to go to leaf, and the heads of blooms that are produced become large and ungainly looking.

As far as singles are concerned, the range is very wide and especially good are 'Paul Crampel' and its salmon form; 'Victory', 'Maxim Kovalevski' and

Fig. 2a. Semi-double flowers of differing formation   Fig. 2b Fully double flower

'Notting Hill Beauty', the latter having distinct zonal marks on the rich dark green leaves. All bedding geraniums need not be of such strong colours and 'Mrs. E. G. Hill', a delightful pink, is most pleasing, whilst some of the ivy-leaved sorts including 'Madame Crousse' have flowers with most delicate colour tones.

So much depends upon the other subjects which are being bedded with geraniums as to the exact varieties chosen. It is certainly possible to find happy associates for the geranium, either in the form of dot plants of the same height, or taller subjects such as standard fuchsias in named varieties, or *Abutilon thompsonii* with its pale green, yellow variegated foliage.

Grey-leaved plants also set off geraniums well. Among the most useful subjects for this purpose, is *Cineraria maritima*, which has handsome silvery leaves. It is comparatively hardy, standing up to rough treatment in the way of weather. There is a particularly fine form known as Diamond, which has broad snow-white foliage. The taller growing *Verbena venosa* with its purple-blue flowers, also produces a striking effect when bedded with geraniums. Used in conjunction with a variety such as 'Decorator', and with blue petunias as ground cover, a happy association is produced.

Geraniums can also be used as dot plants in other planting schemes, and many possibilities will suggest themselves as one inspects the beds laid out in some of our parks. Variegated bedding geraniums are attracting more interest and there are some having green leaves edged ivory-white, such as 'Flower of Spring'.

'A Happy Thought' has an ivory centre with a wide green edging and produces single rose flowers. This variety is sometimes known as butterfly zoned, due to the irregular shaped ivory blotch in the centre. 'Harry Hieover' has greenish-yellow leaves with a dark brown zone, while 'Mrs. Quilter' has yellowish leaves with a reddish-pink zone. The foliage of 'Crystal Palace Gem' is a yellowish shade with a marked green centre.

Of the tricolours 'Mrs. Pollock' and 'Mrs. H. Cox' find favour in many bedding schemes, because of the irregular markings of red, yellow and green. Sometimes the almost black foliaged 'Black Vesuvius' is used, although these plants are comparatively weak in growth and should therefore be kept for edging. Once established they often flower so freely that they weaken themselves.

Standard Geraniums

Very often it is helpful and an improvement to have taller growing subjects in beds or borders of geraniums, and while such items as abutilons and fuchsias are generally used, it is not difficult to produce standard geraniums, which can greatly contribute to an outstanding display not only in public parks but in ordinary gardens. Standard geraniums, in fact, are just as easy to grow as the normal bedding sized plants, the only difference being that the cuttings must be struck earlier and the resultant plants kept during the following winter in a temperature of not less than 55 deg. F. (13 C.).

Really good specimens, with large, shapely heads, take two seasons to form and by that time, it should be possible to have outstanding plants with stems varying from two to three feet. The normal procedure is to take short jointed cuttings 4 or 5 inches long during July, selecting these from strong, healthy parent plants which are free from infection of any kind.

Any plant showing the slightest signs of spotted or otherwise marked foliage should be avoided, in order that standards are not trained from material affected by virus and similar troubles. Sometimes, the foliage of plants shows chlorotic spots. These turn yellow and often become quite brown. In many cases, the leaves pucker and the plant is generally sickly looking. Later however, such plants often seem to recover and appear to be normal and healthy, but it is most unwise to take cuttings from such specimens.

After the lower leaves and stipules have been removed and a clean cut has been made with a sharp knife, immediately below a leaf joint, they are inserted in sandy compost in the usual way. Once the small pots are full of roots, the

Ready for planting out   *Photo Wilson Bros. U.S.A.*

young plants are moved to bigger pots using the John Innes Compost No. 2 or something similar. All side growths must be pinched out and at this stage it is a good plan to give the rooted cuttings the support of a thin cane, so that the central growing point can be trained upright.

Not all growers will want a standard with the same size stem, and although the requirement of a 28-inch stem laid down by the Geranium Society for its competitions is an excellent guide, it is of course possible to restrict the stem to whatever height is preferred. It is most important to train the stem with great care from the earliest stages, so that it grows straight and this means early staking and regular tying.

All varieties do not make satisfactory standards and generally speaking, it is best to stick to the strongest growing zonal sorts such as 'Decorator', 'Gustav Emich' and 'Paul Crampel'. Although I have never attempted it, it is certainly possible to graft slender stemmed varieties on to the named sorts just mentioned. In this case, one would need to select with great care because of the probable natural differences in the thickness of the stems of the two sorts. It is even probable that plants of the ivy-leaved section could be grafted on to the stem of a zonal variety. In this way a more or less weeping standard would be produced. It might also be possible to train certain varieties into odd shapes, although such action would not be to everyone's liking.

54

Bedding Out

Before bedding out geraniums on a large scale it is advisable to make up your mind on what sort of effect is desired. Much will depend on the size and position of the bed. Bright colours such as the showy scarlet 'Paul Crampel' should not be planted in quantity where they will be constantly before the eyes. Neither should a bed of vividly contrasting colours. Pinks and whites should be used more; certainly in a small garden they give a more pleasing effect than the glaring scarlets, and the purple and magenta coloured varieties.

Where very bright colours are used in large beds, a more attractive display is secured if a less brilliant variety is planted towards the edge of the bed. This tones down any harshness and prevents an abrupt termination to the display, making it easier on the eyes. Whilst it is unwise to use too many different varieties in the same bed or border a really large-scale planting, skilfully designed and placed, can be made to look like a beautiful carpet. One must however, discern the correct relationships between the harmonies of colour and scale.

If you wish to find in your garden quietness and soothing, use the softer reds, pinks and whites, and plant the coloured-leaved varieties freely. If however, you want to find inspiration and encouragement for action, the scarlet 'Paul Crampel', 'Gustav Emich', 'Beatrix Little' and 'Vera Dillon' will goad you on.

Stellar Geraniums

This fairly new race produced in America was first distributed as Pelargonium staphysagroides, but as has now been discovered, they bear no resemblance to this species. The plants have star-shaped foliage, some deeply zoned.

Stellar varieties have single or double flowers held high above the foliage on erect stems. The lower petals are broad and wedge-shaped with a serrated edge, the upper petals being narrower and forked.

Good cultivars include: 'Dawn Star', single pink; 'Grenadier', double scarlet; 'Pixie Fire', deep red, white eye, and 'Snowflake', white.

6 Pots, Tubs, Baskets and Window Boxes

THE SIGHT of a few floral decorations, such as window-boxes and hanging baskets, adorning public buildings and private houses is always welcome. There should be much more of this commendable use of flowers, and gardeners and nurserymen might pay more attention to publicizing gardening by these methods.

Many large industrial and other firms employ a local nurseryman on contract, to keep their window-boxes furnished throughout the year, and where labour and supplies of plants are available, this could surely be extended, with profit and improvement to the general appearance of the surroundings.

Those who have not had much experience of erecting and constructing window-boxes, should give the matter a little thought beforehand. It is of little use to make a box of wood that is so thin that after a few weeks of watering, the whole thing collapses. The wood should be at least $\frac{3}{4}$ inch thick, and preferably 1 inch. Some char the interiors of the boxes by burning shavings or the like inside, but on the whole I prefer to apply a chemical preservative such as those used for frame lights. On no account should creosote be used for this purpose, for it is more than likely to cause trouble with the plants grown in the box afterwards.

The depth of the window-box should be 8 inches or more and its width at least 7 inches. If the dimensions have to be less than those suggested, then the soil will dry out rather readily and watering will have to be more frequent. Moreover, the amount of soil contained in the box will be less, and the plants may become short of food, unless regular top-dressings of organic fertilizers are applied. The length of the box will depend on the length of the sill, but where these are wide it might be worth-while to make two short boxes to stand side by side. These half-size boxes would be easier and lighter to handle especially when filled with soil.

Most window-sills slope outwards towards the street and so the window-box must be fitted with suitable wedges so that it stands level. This is essential, partly because otherwise the box may slide off the sill and also because uniform and even watering is not possible if the box slopes one way. Too much emphasis cannot be placed on the need to make the boxes quite secure in position on the window-sill. The wedges if needed, will help to make the box sit level and safe, but in addition, it is a good precaution to secure each box to the house with small iron brackets screwed to the box and to the timber window-frame, or to fix a strong wire around the box and attach it to the house.

The bottom of the box will be kept a little raised above the sill by the wedges, so that this will also assist the drainage of surplus water from the box. A gap beneath the box in this way and also perhaps at the back of the box between the box and the house wall, will allow a current of air around it and help to prevent rot. Such boxes are often wider than the sill. A small overhang is quite all right providing the box is really secured safely. The provision of drainage holes at the bottom of the box is an obvious necessity and they may be $\frac{1}{2}$ inch in diameter and spaced 6 or 8 inches apart, usually in two rows.

Years ago window-boxes were faced with oak bark for ornamentation which made them look very attractive. This adds to the cost, however, and although it looks specially well in the depth of winter, when filled with plants during the summer months, the presence of trailing plants over the sides of the box is adequate to conceal any plain wood.

The roots of the plants growing in the box will naturally be very restricted and therefore the compost should be fairly rich, so that the plants are not starved. Something equivalent to the John Innes Potting Compost No. 2 is ideal. The inclusion of some fertilizer, preferably a well-balanced compound, containing organics – such as hoof and horn meal – is especially important.

Crocks over the drainage holes and some lumpy material or pieces of turf at the bottom will normally be placed in position before the soil. When the boxes have to be erected on window-sills which are difficult of access, or at high elevation, it may be preferable to place the empty boxes in position and then add the soil and plants afterwards. There is something to be said for filling the boxes with plants growing in pots, plunging the pots in moist peat to reduce the loss of water from the soil. These plants can readily be changed for fresh ones but they need more frequent watering and are not likely to make such big plants as those planted in boxes filled with soil.

Watering is best done in the morning or late at night especially where the boxes are in such a position that moisture might drip on passers by. Occasional liquid feeds and the removing of dead and fading flowers will ensure a continuity of display.

Window-boxes need never be empty for when geraniums have finished their showy display by October, daffodils, narcissus, tulips and wallflowers can be planted and these will provide a colourful show in the spring before the geraniums are planted again.

Geraniums in Hanging Baskets

Hanging baskets look delightful in porchways or overhanging verandahs and similar places. In addition, they are sometimes used very effectively by town councils or other public bodies for street decoration.

Perhaps the most important point in securing entirely satisfactory results is to line the basket with moss or similar material which will keep the soil within the basket and give a firm base for the plants used. For soil, the John Innes Compost No. 2 is very suitable and especially so if a saucer containing charcoal is placed in the basket before any soil is added. It is important to ensure that the hook or support used will stand the weight of the filled basket, which is really heavy after it has been watered.

In this connection, it is not satisfactory to water the hanging basket with a watering can, for then the moisture will just run off. It is far better to take down the basket and immerse it in a bath or pail of water until it is well soaked. Then allow it to drain off before returning the basket to its proper place.

57

There are many interesting and showy geraniums which can be used, and for trailing the ivy-leaved varieties are invaluable, especially 'Charles Turner' and 'Galilee', used either by themselves or combined with *Asparagus sprengeri*, *tradescantia*, trailing lobelia, nepeta, periwinkles, nasturtiums and *Linaria cymbalaria*.

Since for hanging baskets it is essential to select plants which have a long flowering period, the zonal geraniums are easily the first choice for under

Window Box   *Photo H. Smith*

58

Wall Basket   *Photo H. Smith*

ordinary circumstances they will flower outdoors from the end of May until
October. Such sorts as 'Paul Crampel', 'Gustav Emich' and 'King of Denmark'
seem able to withstand all the vagaries of our summer weather including winds
which shrivel most other subjects.

While various kinds of baskets may be employed, the wire type is certainly
the cheapest, an added advantage being that plants such as *Helxine solierolii*
or Selaginella can be worked in among the moss used for lining. Do not finish
off the basket with a mound of soil, for this makes proper watering impossible.

Although the geraniums already mentioned are well tried, dependable
favourites, any effect made to provide a wider colour range than the usual
pinks and reds, will be well repaid. In this connection, many of the variegated
foliaged sorts can be employed. Among the best of these for the purpose of
providing arresting colour combinations are: 'Mrs. Quilter', with its chestnut
zone and pink flowers, planted with 'Galilee' one of the best pink ivy-leaved
varieties; 'Caroline Schmidt', double scarlet flowers and silver leaves, with
one of the scarlet Ivies such as 'Sir Percy Blakeney' in front; 'Lady Churchill'
or 'Chelsea Gem', with its fine silver leaves and double pink flowers, and the
ivy-leaved pink flowered 'Charles Turner'.

Another simple yet effective idea, is to plant up a number of sweet-scented-
leaved sorts, for with these there is not only a variety of perfume, but a great
variation in the colour and shape of the foliage. This sort of box is perhaps   **59**

most suitable for the conservatory or the inside of a living-room. It is well worth repeating that whatever boxes or baskets are used, regular supplies of moisture are necessary, and an extra quantity of peat or leaf mould added to the growing compost will help to prevent rapid drying out.

Geraniums in Pots

Geraniums in pots do best if the pots are small for the size of the plants. They will grow into fairly large plants, actually small shrubs, if they have a lot of root room. They will stay smaller and flower much more freely if kept potbound. A 4-inch pot is large enough for indoor plants. Larger pots may be used on porches or terraces if the plant is large enough for the pot. Never put a small plant in a large pot, but change sizes by stages as the plants grow.

Potting soil for geraniums should be of a texture to give good drainage and aeration, but of sufficient body to allow firm potting. Ideally it should be slightly acid.

A wide variety of soil mixtures has been recommended and used successfully for geraniums. Apparently, the preferences and habits of the grower are as important as the requirements of the plants! Any soil that gives good results is suitable soil, and in such cases, there is not much point in trying other mixtures. Actually the soil mixture is not at all vital. Rather heavy soils with a low proportion of organic material are generally considered best for geraniums. Such simple mixtures as two parts garden soil and one part coarse sand or three parts garden soil, one part coarse sand, and one part peat moss are good. The amount of sand to use depends upon the quality of the garden soil. The suggested amounts are for a medium heavy clay loam. More sand should be used with heavy clay loams, less with lighter soils of small clay content. The soil should be a little moist when potting. It is difficult to pot properly with soil that is either too dry or too wet.

Before potting, a little soil should be scraped from the top of the root ball to remove any moss or algae on the surface, and a little soil should be crumpled from the top and bottom shoulders of the ball to loosen some of the roots. If the soil is dry and hard, it can be moistened a little for this operation, but care should be taken that the soil does not become so wet that the ball falls to pieces. The plants should be potted a little deeper than they were grown, but no leaf stalks should be buried. The potting should be firm. A small stick may be used to press the new soil around the original ball. The finished soil level should be about $\frac{1}{2}$ inch below the rim of the 3-inch pot. The first watering must be thorough enough to soak all of the soil, both new and old. If the water runs through very rapidly, more should be given, so that it is certain that all of the original soil is wet.

Potted geraniums cannot be watered to rule. They should be watered only when it is needed. They need lots of moisture when they are growing well under favourable conditions. It is best to water geraniums thoroughly and to allow the soil to get moderately dry before watering again. Geraniums do not wilt quickly when they are dry, so that it is necessary to judge moisture by the appearance and feel of the soil.

Serious damage may occur if the soil is allowed to get too dry. Such damage appears a day or two later with a sudden yellowing (and eventual loss) of the lower leaves. In extreme cases, all of the roots and the lower part of the stem may be killed. Such plants continue to grow at the top for a time, but eventually rot at the base. Young plants, and some of the fancy-leaved and dwarf varieties are most easily damaged by lack of water. Since the soil in small pots dries out quickly, the plants should be looked at often. Watering from the top of the soil is better and easier than watering from below. Enough water should be given so that a little drains through the pot. Water should not be allowed to remain in a saucer under the pot.

Geraniums do best in a cool soil. In summer the pots should be shaded from sun. One way to do this is to set the potted plants in a second pot one or two sizes larger, so that there is a shaded air space between the two pots.

Usually the common red clay flower pots are best for geraniums since they provide good aeration and cool soil. In positions where the plants dry out very quickly, glazed pots help to retain moisture. Either kind of pot can be used successfully anywhere, but the watering has to be adjusted to allow for the difference in evaporation loss.

Potted geraniums will need feeding sooner or later. Need of plant food is indicated when the leaves are a paler green than normal and the flowers become smaller. It is best to use one of the complete or organic balanced fertilizers. Applications should be made only as often as needed, and not oftener than once a month, unless the need is very evident. Too frequent or too large applications may damage or kill the plant. Brands of fertilizer may be stronger or weaker, and the instructions of the maker should be followed. There are now available a number of fertilizers which are dissolved in water and applied as liquid. These are convenient and effective. The maker's instructions should be read carefully, since these fertilizers are generally quite strong. It is often best to use smaller doses than are recommended for these fertilizers, for geraniums are better when not fed too richly.

Zonal pelargoniums make first-class permanent pot plants, though some varieties are better than others for this purpose. Care is needed in the choice of plants for pots, whether they are to be grown in the living-room or green-house. Many varieties which are first class for bedding because of the vigour and large foliage, are not so suitable for pots or vases. For instance, 'Paul Crampel', 'King of Denmark' and 'Mrs. E. K. Hill', whilst splended for bedding, are too coarse growing for indoor use.

Fig. 3.   Typical single flowers of zonal pelargonium

For this purpose, habit of growth must be considered. A plant which will grow stocky, with short internodes and which branches freely, is the type to concentrate on for the window-sill or greenhouse. The majority will flower consistently over a long period if kept under good light conditions. When grown outdoors, very large heads or trusses of blooms are often formed, the individual flowers being fairly small. In contrast, many indoor grown plants

61

Geraniums in pots

Photo H. Smith

produce fewer but larger and better shaped, individual flowers on each truss.

There is no need to grow the more glaring scarlet, pink or orange varieties in pots, for there is a wide range of varieties of the softer shades of red, coral and salmon as well as the bicolours and fancy varieties to choose from. In addition, the scented leaved varieties, miniature, variegated and other unusual sorts, are well worth concentrating upon.

The variegated-leaved forms, with their contrasting colours merit special consideration. Some of these are of a definite dwarf habit. 'Mrs. Quilter' always looks well, its dainty yellowish-green leaves having a pink zone, which matures to a chestnut colour. Then there are the pelargonium species, some of which are architecturally pleasing. 'Salmonia' is an example. Although slow growing, it will sometimes make quite big plants. The small, zoned, dentate leaves are dark green, the flowers being thin petalled, and of a warm salmon or coral-pink shade. These are produced on wiry stems held well above the foliage.

'Skelly's Pride' (Flame) is also interesting for pots. Although slow growing, it sometimes develops a straggly habit. The leaves are a glossy dark green, the single orange-pink flowers having petals with serrated edges. Not very easy to obtain, red 'Black Vesuvius' is a true miniature geranium, forming a compact bush, rarely exceeding 9 or 10 inches in height. The small, very dark green leaves have a broad black zone, and contrast markedly with the single, signal-red flowers.

'Skies of Italy' also makes a good pot plant. It is of neat habit, the green leaves with pointed lobes, margined creamy yellow, being zoned brownish-red. The small single flowers are scarlet.

Geraniums do best if the pots are on the small side. If they have too much root room they may become quite large, a quality not required for indoor plants. Kept with a fairly restricted root space they will remain compact and flower much more freely, or in the case of the ornamental foliage sorts, the colours will be much more intensive.

The plants can be moved to bigger-sized pots as growth develops. To place a small plant in a large pot of soil in which there are few roots, leads to the compost becoming sour. It is normally satisfactory to put the plants in 3-inch pots when received from the grower, and when they are well established and growing freely, they can be moved to the next largest size pot.

Apart from the more usual pots, urns and tubs may be used for growing geraniums for brightening verandahs, roof gardens, terraces and porches. The pendant habit of the ivy-leaved varieties can be exploited to the full, since the stems can be allowed to grow loosely over the edges of the containers, lessening any suggestion of formality.

Perhaps one of the most undesirable things which occurs with geraniums permanently grown in pots is the algae or green growth which frequently develops on the outside of the receptacles. This proves detrimental to the

Hanging Basket   *Photo H. Smith*

63

appearance of the plants, whether in the greenhouse, living-room or when being sent to the market. It has been the practice of commercial growers and others to get rid of the algae which occurs on pots in greenhouses, by spraying with one of the copper compounds.

This cannot altogether be recommended, however, since such spraying does retard normal root development, and in some cases has led to definite injury to plant life. At the best, the upset of the roots by the solution workings its way through the walls of the pots makes it perhaps best to avoid these copper solutions.

For the average small grower, the simplest way of keeping the outside of the pots clean, is to give them occasional rubbings over with soap and water.

Although most plants grow in the 3- or 4-inch pots, sometimes when they are lifted from their summer bedding positions it is necessary to give them a bigger size.

An improvement in the potential of geranium pot plant production has been achieved with the introduction of a growth regulant. Known as Phosfon, its application has been found to avoid leggy plants with little bloom and poor general appearance.

The resultant reduction in size of the plants and the earlier bud initiation, produces a stocky, well balanced, short jointed plant. The following are claimed to be the advantages of the use of Phosfon. Controlled growth rate; increased botrytis resistance; improved colour; greater resistance to drought; sturdier habit and prolonged flower life.

Phosfon is a powder, directions for use being fully given on the containers.

One problem of growing geraniums and pelargoniums in pots, although perhaps not a major one, is that it is sometimes difficult to ensure that the plants have sufficient moisture if one intends being away for a period and it is not possible for anyone to attend to watering. If your absence from home is likely to exceed a week some steps must be taken to provide a slow but continuous supply of water and there are several methods of doing this.

One simple and most satisfactory way is to use a wide lamp wick, which has not previously been used for its normal purpose. One end of this should be placed in a bucket of water and the other end placed under the plant pots. The volume of water can of course, be controlled by the size of the wick.

Another method is to attach a piece of alkathene tube to the water tap, and train the tube over each of the pots, the tube being punctured with a small hole over each pot. By varying the size of the holes in the tube and the volume of water from the tap, you will be able to control the amount reaching the plant. This apparatus, and the plants, should, of course, be placed where adequate drainage of the surplus water can be provided.

The systems described suffer from one common failing, and that is that the plants being themselves unable to say how much water they want, there is a risk that they may become too saturated. Great care should be exercised to ensure that this does not take place, by reducing the flow of water to the absolute minimum, and on your return do see that all plants so treated are drained off well and that the earth is allowed to return to its normal moisture content before resuming your own particular method of watering.

Those who have wick-fed pots should have no worries whilst they are away, providing that the container of water is sufficiently large. This system, which consists of a small diameter wick, one end of which is unravelled and spread over the bottom of the flower pot, the other end being placed in a suitable container of water, is one which can be readily made in the house.

Sometimes plants can be stood on bricks placed in the bottom of the bath, which should be filled with water to just below the level of the top of the bricks. This will provide a nice humid atmosphere, but it is doubtful whether the plants will receive an adequate supply of water.

My last method relies on conserving the water in the soil and preventing it from evaporating. First of all the plants should be given a thoroughly good soaking, and they should then be placed in an air-tight miniature greenhouse made out of polythene, sealed at the edges by the usual lighted match method. The size of the 'greenhouse' will depend on the number of plants it is to contain–if only one, then a polythene bag will be satisfactory. Care should be exercised, however, to drain off surplus water from the plant before placing it (or them) in the polythene container in order to avoid risk of mildew or damping off.

Do make sure that all of your plants are disease- and insect-free. Four days before you go away give them a thorough wash with insecticide and three days after this give them all another insecticide spray. Any diseased plants such as those suffering from fungicidal diseases or eelworm should be thrown away, or better still burned, in order to prevent the spread of the disease or the eelworms to the other plants.

Bottled Geraniums

A novel way of growing geraniums is in hanging bottles, a method which has been described as Bottled Geraniums. For this one should take a dark green quart bottle, one having a 'kick' at the base, and knock a hole, about $\frac{3}{4}$ inch in diameter, in the centre of the 'kick'. Then insert two or three rooted cuttings of a fairly vigorous grower like 'Paul Crampel' into the hole, i.e. the cuttings are upside down but they will soon tend to turn up following the sides of the bottle, especially with a little judicious pruning. Now, through the top of the bottle, put in John Innes Potting Compost No. 2, until it is about three-quarters full; then water through the neck end of the bottle.

Wire firmly round the neck and hang up the bottle by an S-hook. No claim is made for artistic merit, but the bottles have found favour with public houses–the stipulation being that the label is left intact. Thus adornment and advertisement are achieved.

Pelargonium Carousel   *Photo Wilson Bros, U.S.A.*

7 Zonal Pelargoniums

TO MANY PEOPLE 'geranium' means the plant bearing showy scarlet flowers, so often used for summer bedding or for growing in a pot on the window-sill. Yet the pelargonium, which is the official name for the plant we usually refer to as a geranium, is very diverse in form and habit. It is only as one becomes really interested in these plants that one realizes how extensive is the range of varieties available.

Zonal Pelargoniums

For convenience, there are seven main divisions generally recognized among specialists and collectors. They are: 1, Zonal Geraniums; 2, Ivy-leaf Geraniums; 3, Scented-leaf Geraniums; 4, Regal or Show Pelargoniums; 5, Species Pelargonium; 6, Miniature Geraniums; 7, All other Pelargoniums which cannot be fitted into the other five sections.

Easily the most popular and widely grown are the zonal varieties. It is these that can be seen freely planted in gardens and public parks during the summer. The epithet, zonal, is perhaps somewhat misleading, since although it originally referred to a zone or band of a darker colour found on the leaves of the earlier varieties, there are very many named zonal geraniums which have no zone at all, and in others it is very, very faint. It is also a fact that there are some geraniums which have zoned leaves, but belong to another section.

The zonal varieties are now referred to officially as *Pelargonium hortorum* cultivars, and the original varieties were the result of a cross between *Pelargonium zonale* and *P. inquinans*. The dark horseshoe shaped marking on the leaves of the original varieties are responsible for their common name of Horseshoe Geraniums.

As is to be expected since zonal geraniums have been grown and have continually increased in popularity for a period of approaching 150 years, many thousands of varieties have been raised, both in Britain and abroad. Some have had a fleeting existence, others have stayed the course, and have remained and increased in favour for very many years.

Pelargonium Decorator   *Photo H. Smith*

Some are of a compact habit of growth, others are inclined to make spreading stems. Some have large, heavy heads, others have shapely, medium sized trusses of flowers. There are those with single flowers and many more with semi-double or fully double blooms. Lists of varieties are somewhat dangerous for no two enthusiasts are likely to include exactly the same sorts in their selection. The fact that it would be possible to make out several lists of different first-class varieties is an indication of the embarrassment of riches there is to be found in these satisfying plants.

It would be difficult, of course, to select only a dozen varieties as being the best, for one might be influenced in their choosing by how well a particular variety had behaved during the last season. Then there are some, such as 'Lady Warwick', which, although having smaller flower trusses, produce them in such abundance that one fears they may flower themselves to death. It is also difficult to choose between 'Maxim Kovalevsky' and 'Sansovino', although the former usually secures most votes. The list which follows later in this chapter, whilst reasonably comprehensive, does not claim to include all reliable varieties in cultivation today.

Pelargoniums are quite happy during the winter months, with a temperature of just over 40 deg. F. (6 C.). Really high temperatures are unnecessary since the object should be to ensure good stock plants of compact habit. This also means that the plants should not be overcrowded in any way, and they should be so placed in the greenhouse that they are not drawn towards the light. If they are, they will become tall, pale and spindly.

Whether one is growing just a few plants for greenhouse or conservatory decoration, or considerably larger quantities for bedding out during the summer, stocks should be looked over during January. At that time, there will usually be two types of plants available, the older specimens, or stools, perhaps up to four or five years old, and the cuttings taken the previous September.

It is usually possible to pot up the cuttings individually, and well before Christmas. The job should certainly not be delayed until later than the end of January. Although the potted cuttings can be placed fairly close together in the first instance, once the leaves begin to develop and are touching each other, the pots should be given more space, so that the air can circulate freely around the plants.

By the end of February, these young plants should be growing freely, and then it is the time to stop them. Sometimes the piece taken out is of sufficient size to make an additional cutting. The remaining stock plant should have at least four or five leaves on it, and by the end of May, a fresh shoot will have been produced making a sturdy plant. By that time it is quite usual for the first flower to be opening, with several buds following in close succession. Such specimens will make an immediate show if bedded out towards the end of May, or early June.

When cuttings are taken early in the year, greenhouse space is usually short, but a number of tip cuttings can be rooted in pans or seed trays. If a propagating frame is available, so much the better, particularly if bottom heat is provided. Within a week or so these young cuttings, under good conditions, will have commenced rooting, and they can then be placed on the greenhouse shelf in full light, where they will develop slowly and make compact plants.

These young plants can be left in the boxes and planted directly into garden beds. Being small they will do excellently for edging beds of taller growing plants. Tip cuttings of this type are also useful where stocks are in short supply of any particular variety, or in the case of new or rare sorts.

Zonal geraniums are among the most rewarding of bedding plants, and will go on giving a continuous and brilliant display from the time they are planted out until there is danger of early frosts, towards the end of September. They will certainly give better results if grown under good conditions, for in spite of the belief in some quarters that geraniums thrive in poor soil, there is no doubt at all that they do best when given liberal treatment and good soil with a high humus content.

It is when the quick acting fertilizers are applied either in the pots or beds, that growth becomes quick and thin, subsequently leading to indifferent results.

How the famous zonal geranium 'Paul Crampel' was introduced is rarely told. Nearly seventy years ago, the man whose name this variety bears was a nurseryman at Nancy, France. In a batch of seedlings there appeared an unusual looking plant which obviously showed great possibilities, and being a shrewd man, Paul Crampel did not take long to assess its value.

He built up a large stock from that one plant, although it is said that he did not reveal what he was doing to any of his employees or anyone else. He took great care in keeping the plants under his personal supervision, carefully and regularly removing the flower buds before they showed colour, lest someone should guess his find, and some of his plants be removed.

He sold many plants for 20s. or more each, so that it did not take long to make a very handsome sum of money. Today this same variety is still really important, especially where clean virus-free stocks are grown, and one should always insist on having the true stock, and not some other light scarlet which is frequently distributed as 'Paul Crampel'.

In spite of all that has been said during the last few decades against this variety, it is very doubtful whether there is any other flowering subject which is so suited for the beds of small gardens, particularly in town and industrial areas. What other plant is there which will keep a garden so gay all the summer, at so little cost, and with the minimum of attention, or which will stand up to adverse weather conditions?

Just as there is a legend about rosemary, and the way its flowers turned blue after Mary, the Mother of Christ, hung her robes to dry on a rosemary bush, so there is an Eastern legend concerning the geranium. It is one of Moslem origin and connected with the marsh mallow.

This particular mallow was, so the tale runs, the only plant of its kind. One day the prophet Mohammed was taking his customary walk, when he found himself in unfrequented country. It was very hot. The sun was shining fiercely on his body. To obtain relief he took off his shirt, and rinsed it in a nearby pool around which grew a quantity of marshmallow plants. After the rinsing, Mohammed hung the garment on the branches of an overhanging tree to dry. As it hung there, water from the shirt dripped down on to one of the mallows which immediately turned into a most beautiful geranium plant, while the other mallows growing around the pool retained their original form.

Irene Geraniums

During the last twenty years, much has been heard of the Irene strain of zonal pelargoniums.

They do equally well inside or out of doors and are naturally self branching, the plants being bushier than the normal zonal varieties. They are excellent for winter flowering, and for this purpose cuttings should be taken in spring. Pinch out the flower buds until September after which the plants may be allowed to develop normally.

A temperature of around 60 deg. F. (16 C.) is required with plenty of daylight. Among the earliest varieties were Cal, salmon-pink; Genie, soft red, and Penny, purplish-pink with occasional streaks of white. All are semi-double with large florets borne on strong stems and frequently carrying twenty-five or more flowers per stem.

Since these varieties were introduced a number of other really first class sorts have been raised including La Jolla, an unusual shade of crimson; Modesty, white; Party Dress pale pink; Topscore, brick-red; Treasure Chest, luminous orange-red with cupped petals and Trulls Hatch, coral pink.

Experience has shown that under wet weather conditions these plants show a tendency to lose their compact habit; also the blooms do not stand up too well to the continuous wet. When outside conditions are drier, plantings made in various aspects on poor soil give normal growth and flower production is satisfactory, but where plantings are made on rich soil and in partial shade, growth is often rapid at the expense of flower production.

Equally good results come from Irene geraniums planted in tubs, window-boxes and similar confined spaces, where they flower in profusion from May to October. All varieties have been tested for their cut-flower value and, without exception, proved themselves remarkably satisfactory, lasting in water from ten to fifteen days.

Lists of plant names can be tiring to read and in making up any list there is always the probability that some good varieties will be omitted or the favourite varieties of a certain grower disregarded. Even so, lists do give some guidance, and while it is not claimed that the following is in any way a complete table of all the best varieties, it does contain the names of many of the finest and most important zonal pelargoniums. A few of those mentioned may be difficult to locate at the present time, but nearly all of them can be obtained from specialist growers.

The single flowered group have normally no more than five petals. The semi-double and double flowered varieties usually have six or more petals, although they do not form a centre or heart like the bud of a rose.

Mature plants of the Zonal varieties normally grow more than 8 inches high. When they are shorter than this, they are usually classed as miniatures. They are of course, grown chiefly for their flowers and in cases where the petals are quilled or twisted, they are referred to as cactus-flowered geraniums.

Red, Scarlet and Crimson

BEATRIX LITTLE, a recent introduction, making a lovely plant up to 8 inches high, with very effective, single scarlet flowers freely produced.

CAPTAIN FLAYELLE, an excellent bedder, with large crimson-scarlet flowers of good quality.

CAROLINE SCHMIDT. Double scarlet flowers, silver variegated foliage.

COLONEL DRABBE. Double crimson, with a small white centre.

COUNTESS OF BIRKENHEAD. Scarlet with large flowers and heads.

70

Irene Geranium Penny   *Photo H. Bagust*   71

DECORATOR, a really first-class semi-double, crimson-scarlet, a strong grower and excellent for bedding.

DORIS MOORE. A well-tried, reliable cherry-red variety.

DRUMMER BOY. Vermilion, small white eye, good grower.

DRYDEN. Free flowering, the scarlet-red flowers having darker lower petals.

ELIZABETH CARTWRIGHT A.M., R.H.S. 1950. Carmine-red with small white eye. Very suitable for bedding and greenhouse work.

EVENING MAIL (BENNETT). A superb brilliant bright red. Large trusses freely produced.

F. V. RASPAIL. A long grown and reliable sort, with scarlet flowers which last well. A small grower, but admirable for bedding purposes.

FORTYNINER. Brilliant red, of good habit.

GUSTAV EMICH. An old variety of great value which was once widely known as the Buckingham Palace Geranium, on account of its being planted extensively on the gardens near the Palace. The semi-double scarlet blooms are continuous in their appearance.

HENRY JACOBY DOUBLE. Another old favourite with dark red flowers.

JOHN MUIR. Double red of dwarf habit.

LAWRENCE JOHNSTONE. Currant-red of dwarf habit.

MRS. EDDOWES. Large; deep velvety orange-red, with small white eye.

MILLFIELD RIVAL, strong growing, producing giant heads of rose-pink.

PANDORA. Geranium-lake, vigorous growing.

PAUL CRAMPEL. The most popular reliable scarlet variety.

PRESIDENT BAILLER. Semi-double brick-red; showy.

ROSEMARY. Mandarin-red, vary large flowers.

RED BLACK VESUVIUS. Must be included here, for although it is dwarf, growing only about six inches high, it produces its showy scarlet blooms in great quantities, and has very dark, almost black foliage.

RYECROFT PRIDE, one of the very best deep crimson sorts.

SENSATION. Turkestan bright red, small white eye.

STANSTED. Pillar-box-red, white base.

VICTORIOUS. This is really an extra large, fine form of 'Paul Crampel'.

WILLINGDON BEAUTY. Rich Indian-lake.

Pink, Salmon and Rose shades

AUDREY. Good-sized trusses of semi-double, soft rose-pink.

BARBARA HOPE. Soft rich pink. Shapely plants.

CHELSEA GEM. Referred to under the variegated-leaved sorts.

DOT SLADE. Soft salmon-rose, single, greenhouse variety.

ERIC HOSKINS. Perfectly formed pale pink, salmon centre.

FLOWERFIELD. Bright cerise with white eye.

FRENCH BOUQUET. A strong growing variety with small camellia-rose flowers.

GARIBALDI. Large double, soft salmon-pink.

HARMONY. Deep salmon, single flowers.

HUGO DE VRIES. Double peach-pink.

KING OF DENMARK. Deservedly popular with large trusses of semi-double salmon-pink on sturdy, short-jointed plants.

LADY ELLENDEN. Large semi-double, shiny rose-pink.

LADY FOLKESTONE. Fuschine-pink, with white eye.

LIEF. Soft orange-pink, of dwarf habit.

MRS. LAWRENCE. Similar to 'Lady Ellenden', but darker.

MRS. E. G. HILL. Single bright satin-pink, good for bedding.

MILLFIELD RIVAL. Strong growing, clear pink with white eye.

NOTTING HILL BEAUTY. Most free flowering, rosey-scarlet.

PINK CRAMPEL. Rose flushed red.

PRINCESS OF WALES. Rather small, single salmon-pink blooms, strong growing.

QUEEN OF DENMARK. A darker shade and stronger growing 'King of Denmark'.

ROSE QUEEN. Large rose-pink flowers with white eye.

SALMON PAUL CRAMPEL, forming very large trusses.

THE SPEAKER. A fine semi-double salmon-pink, first-class for bedding.

White flowered

CRESTA. A fine pure white, single variety.

DOROTHY NAVARRO. Of medium size, with rather flimsy petals, which sometimes are stained light pink.

EDWARD HUMPHRIS. Another old, free flowering white variety. This received an Award of Merit from the R.H.S. in 1953.

GOODWOOD. A very old variety, of rather dwarf habit, and small white flowers.

GARDENIA. A free flowering, satiny white, double sort.

HERMINE or HEROINE. The best double white variety for bedding.

HARLOW PEARL. An attractive variety, the white flowers having a pearl-like sheen.

L'IMMACULE. A good large flowering double white.

MRS. POVEY. Of medium size, and erect habit, the slender stems bearing small flowers, the buds being particularly attractive before they open.

MADAME RECAMIER. Known for over sixty years, this dwarf growing sort freely produces milky-white flowers, which show up well among the tall green foliage.

QUEEN OF WHITES. One of the oldest of all, being of rather dwarf habit but freely producing white flowers.

RYECROFT WHITE. Recorded over seventy years ago, this produces large trusses of paper-white flowers.

STARLIGHT. Excellent as a pot plant when it makes slow bushy growth.

VERITÉ. This bears double white flowers which have a greenish tinge.

WEDDING DAY. Pure white double flowers. Does not 'pink'.

WHITE MAGIC. A semi-double, pure white sort with really large elegant flowers on bushy plants.

WHITE VESUVIUS. A dwarf-growing variety, the deep green leaves having a distinct zone. The flowers are sometimes lightly tinged pink.

There are a number of other varieties such as 'Avalanche', 'Queen of the Belgians' and 'Simplicity', all of which are very similar and are in fact, probably synonymous with some of the other varieties mentioned.

White, marked and fancy

CARMEL. White edged cherry-red.

CHARLES GOUNAUD. Vigorous growing, with full trusses of large white flowers, shaded magenta.

ECSTASY. A dwarf grower with large white flowers flushed rose.

EDELWEISS. A medium-sized flower, veined and irregularly shaded pink.

EMPEROR NICHOLAS. Double white, with carmine edging.

FORTUNE. Double white, margined and flushed pink.

JOY. Double white, margined and flushed salmon-apricot. Variable.

LA CHARITÉ. Double white, mottled pink.

LADY SARAH WILSON. A dwarf growing, free flowering plant, the white flowers being edged and veined red.

LADY WARWICK. White with picotée edge of pink.

LIGHT PAINTED LADY. Single white, with narrow rose-red margin. ˙

MARTELLO. Flushed at base with rose, Good single flowers.

MAURETANIA. White, with pink eye.

MLLE. GAUTHIER. Dwarf growing, with semi-double, pale pink flowers spotted carmine.

NYDIA. Double, creamy-white, rose disc.

PINK SKELLY'S. A dwarf growing free-flowering variety, with medium-sized whitish-pink flowers.

STAPLEGROVE FANCY. Large flowers, edged and spotted pink.

WARLEY. Medium sized flowers veined and edged geranium-red.

WHITE BIRD'S EGG. Dwarf growing free flowering, the small white flowers being edged purple.

WHITEGROVE. Buds pale primrose, opening to white.

XENIA FIELD. Medium sized white flowers, veined scarlet.

Magenta, purple and crimson

A. M. MAYNE. Double purple-crimson, a strong grower. Sometimes listed as 'Purple Emperor' and 'A. Magni', also known as the 'Pickled Cabbage' Geranium.

BELVEDERE GLORY. Magenta-pink, otherwise not unlike 'Paul Crampel'.

BOUGAINVILLEA. Single purple-crimson with white centre.

BROOK'S PURPLE. Double magenta-purple of good form.

FESTIVA MAXIMA. Double purple of excellent quality. Sometimes said to be the same as 'A. M. Mayne', although some blooms at least, lack the crimson shading, resulting in a really fine purple.

GEORGE BURGWIN. Of spreading habit, the small narrow petalled flowers being fuchsia-purple.

LORD CURZON. Vigorous growing, with large trusses of purple shaded red flowers, with white eye.

MAID OF PERTH. Medium sized plants bearing large purple flowers.

PRINCE OF WALES. Of medium size and Tyrian-purple marked flowers.

SIR WINSTON CHURCHILL. Very similar to, if not the same as, 'Lord Curzon'.

STIRLING STENT. Slender stems bearing medium trusses of purple, shaded rose flowers.

THOMAS E. STIMSON. Large clusters of single cerise-crimson.

TITANIA. The medium sized flowers carry full trusses of bright purple-magenta flowers.

VERA DILLON. Medium sized plants, carrying magenta flowers, the upper petals based red.

Zonal Geranium Paul Crampel　　　　　　　　　*Photo H. Smith*

Orange and Orange Salmon

CAMPBELL'S COMET. Intense orange, rather deeper than 'Kovalevski'.

GOLDEN LION. Produces fair sized flowers of orange-pink.

HARVEST MOON. Bushy plants, producing apricot-orange, single flowers.

JANET SCOTT. Upright growing plants carrying medium sized orange, single flowers.

MAXIM KOVALEVSKI. A fine bright, single orange, which keeps its colour well. Ideal for bedding, and a good sort for winter blooming.

ORANGE GEM. Fair sized orange flowers with a white eye.

ORANGESONNE. An outstanding new variety from Switzerland, the rather dwarf plants carrying superb double, orange flowers.

PRINCE OF ORANGE. (Lave.) Dwarf plants with slender stems bearing reddish-orange double flowers.

PROFUSION. Dwarf growing with medium sized orange-red flowers.

75

QUEEN OF ITALY. A delightful single salmon-pink. Extremely free flowering, and makes a good pot plant of excellent shape.

SANSOVINO. A strong grower with large single orange flowers.

Some American growers now offer the zonal geraniums as two distinct types, the standard and the French (or Bruant). The former is the original race of zonals from the well-known parents *P. zonale* and *P. inquinans* and is typified in such well-known examples as 'Maxim Kovalevski' and 'Mrs. Lawrence'.

The first of the Bruant types, which take their names from a French hybridist, appeared in France, apparently as a breakaway from the standard type, about 1880. These are more vigorous in growth and have leaves which are larger, coarser and with more serrated edges. The flower stems are thick, while the irregular flowers have strong, firmly attached petals which do not fall so rapidly as those of the older zonals.

They are, therefore, very suitable for bedding, although most free flowering when grown in pots. In addition, the long-lasting qualities of the flowers make them useful for cutting and general decoration. Not apparently available in this country in quantity at present, there is every reason to believe that they will soon become better known, and when they are, they should soon become popular.

Experience shows that they will not cross readily, if at all, with the standard type of zonal varieties. Good examples of the French or Bruant types are 'Fireglow', orange-scarlet, 'Will Rogers', crimson, 'Orange Ricardo', orange-scarlet, and 'Summer Cloud', white.

8 Regal Pelargoniums

ALTHOUGH it is the Zonal, Sweetly-Scented and Ivy-leaved varieties which receive the most publicity, there is certainly considerable interest in the Regal or Show geraniums. The correct name of these is *Pelargonium domesticum*. The name Regal has its origin in the fact that *Pelargonium domesticum* were largely grown at the royal Sandringham Gardens, and the title was first used in a catalogue issued in 1877 by the once famous geranium firm of Cannels. Although there is no real point in using this title today, it appears to have come to stay. The present-day Regal or Show pelargoniums are reckoned to have been produced as a result of hybridizing a number of species. These include *P. angulosum*, a strong grower which has been known for long over 200 years, *P. cucullatum* and *P. grandiflorum*.

The Show varieties seem always to have been regarded as exclusively greenhouse plants, but they can be, and certainly are, grown outdoors in the flower garden during the summer. When this is done they can be most effective when planted among groups of other subjects; in fact, they give a much more restful appearance than many of the gaudy summer flowering plants sometimes used, especially as the leaves of some sorts are quite attractive even when the plants are out of flower.

Whilst indoors the plants flower to their fullest extent from April to June, if they are given the background of a fence or low wall when planted outdoors, they will be encouraged to keep on blooming. If the flowers are constantly removed when they have passed their best, the supply of colour is prolonged by the regular production of fresh heads.

The construction of the petals is quite different from that of the zonal geraniums, for they are altogether heavier and closer. Perhaps it was their velvety appearance which made these flowers especially attractive to the Victorians. It ought to be said here that the Show or Regal varieties are not naturally winter flowering, and some effort is needed to make them become so. One of the great drawbacks in cultivation is their susceptibility to attacks by green and white fly. When growing in a greenhouse in which there are a variety of subjects, it will be found that the pests always attack these pelargoniums first, and occasionally will not touch any other plants. Details of pest prevention and control will be found in Chapter XVIII.

Regal, Show or Fancy pelargoniums were at one time separate species, but the uniting of several of these caused the distinctive divisions to be lost in the one group of attractive varieties. Popularly known in the United States as

Pelargonium Carisbrooke   *Photo H. Smith*

'Martha' or 'Lady Washington' geraniums, they take in a wide colour range and although their flowering period is shorter than that of zonals, these Show varieties are in many respects, including their shape and beauty, the loveliest of all geraniums.

They make really good specimens and in many cases the velvety textured petals form a flower which is three to four inches or more in diameter. There are some varieties from which the flowers are suitable for using in bouquets and other floral displays, while a well-grown pot plant of any good Regal pelargonium will never fail to prove attractive, especially as there are in most cases several shades of colour in the petals. Since these plants are liable to produce rather taller, longer jointed stems than the zonals, it is a good plan, unless standard or shaped plants are being grown, to maintain a constant supply of young stems by taking cuttings annually. One is thus able to discard plants which have grown lanky or have become otherwise badly shaped. Personally I have found that the best way of keeping plants in good condition is to cut them back hard after they have flowered and when the 'wood' has ripened.

Occasionally, it is as well to root prune as detailed in the chapter on propagation, while a few applications of liquid manure from the time new growth

78

Regal Pelargoniums

commences, early in the year, will be well rewarded by stronger growth and bigger flowers with more brilliant markings.

Plants intended for propagation should have their faded blooms removed before they have an opportunity of setting seeds. They should be placed in full sunshine in the cool greenhouse or frame or even out of doors in a warm, dry position.

The flowers which are produced so freely from well-grown plants can be had in a wide range of attractive colours, in many shades of pink, red-mauve, as well as white. A number of varieties are blotched or rayed on a lighter background. Their time of flowering fortunately fills the gap between the last of the cinerarias and primulas, and the summer flowering pot plants such as begonias and fuchsias.

Show pelargoniums are as easy to grow as the better known zonal type, generally referred to as 'geraniums'.

Just as their flowering time differs from the better known geraniums, so there is some difference in their cultural requirements. Perhaps this is one reason why some growers find slight difficulties, since they attempt to grow both types in the same way. Regal pelargoniums should be grown under cool conditions; they normally begin to flower in early April and usually go out of

Regal Pelargonium Mrs. E. Hickman   *Photo H. Smith*

colour by the end of June. Although their flowering period appears limited, the flowers are really superb, many having a plush-like appearance. The name of regal or show geraniums does them no more than justice, since well-grown plants really do produce a wealth of bloom in a striking colour range.

It is often said and quite honestly believed by even knowledgeable gardeners, that Regal pelargoniums have a short flowering period. This need not be so, for with careful planning, it is possible to have Regals in flower for at least six months of the year, especially if there is room to accommodate the older, larger plants.

To ensure continuity of flowering, it is advisable to take cuttings from the parent plants at odd times, moving them into bigger pots just as they become pot bound. Avoid over potting but give a gradual increase in size of pot according to the demands of growth. In this way, the plants will mature at various times, and when the woody stems ripen they will flower.

It is, by this method, quite easy to spread the flowering period. It is not difficult to take cuttings in relays and if plants have been out of doors during the summer, the first cuttings can be taken when the plants are brought indoors. For this, the side growths are shortened back to the main stem, although when doing so care should be taken to leave at least two or even three, eyes or leaf buds on each remaining spur.

If it is intended that plants should flower from December onwards, they should be brought into a temperature of 55 to 60 deg. F. (13 to 16 C.) and given occasional feeds of some well-balanced fertilizer, preferably of organic origin. In this way, with the later taken cuttings, it will be possible to have a really good display of flowers up until June or even longer.

Pelargoniums are half-hardy and it is best that they should have a rest period. This can be encouraged by withholding water and feeding material. Such treatment will result in partial defoliation and the yellowing of the other leaves. So long as this discoloration is confined to the base of the leaves everything is in order. Once watering and feeding are renewed, the plants soon put out new leaves, and flowers will follow. Although not often done, it is possible with some patience and dexterity, to train Regal pelargoniums on to a framework of stakes and wire. This training can result in fan- or bell-shaped plants, or other designs may be worked out without difficulty.

Regal pelargoniums can certainly be grown out of doors, but cannot be put there until the end of May onwards, according to soil and weather conditions. One of the reasons that they are not grown more out-of-doors is that the large rather heavy blooms are fairly easily damaged by rains and winds. The covering provided by greenhouse, conservatory or loggia is sufficient to give needed protection. It is however, quite a good plan to stand Regal pelargoniums out-of-doors when they have finished their flowering season. This will enable the wood to ripen for the future display of flowers.

A simple way of ensuring that they come to no harm, is to place the pots in ordinary garden soil or peat or leaf mould, plunging them to the rim level of the pots. Adequate water supply must be available so that the roots do not dry out. These plants are of course, brought into a frost-free place early in September.

If you can grow even one or two of these stately pelargoniums, they are well worth any trouble, and such varieties as 'Carisbrooke', soft rose-pink with maroon markings; 'Grand Slam', rich crimson-scarlet; 'Burgundy', wine-red; 'Caprice', carmine-rose; 'Lord Bute', velvety black-carmine with a pictoée edge, and 'Rhodomine', mauve with a white throat, are all dependable. While not by any means new, they have stood the test of time and are altogether reliable.

ANCHURUS. Rose-pink, blotched red, large trusses.

APPLE BLOSSOM. Bright rose-pink on white ground, a vigorous grower.

BLACK BUTTERFLY. Compact short plant, velvety black flower flecked mahogany-red, most outstanding.

BLACK VELVET. Large velvety black upper petals edged purple, the lower purple petals having dull blotches.

BLOSSOMTIME. Frilly pale pink petals shading to almost white.

BLYTHESWOOD. An outstanding show pelargonium. Rich pansy shading to plum with white picotée edge, making a very compact plant.

BONNARD. Introduced 1962. Huge creamy-white boldly flared carmine-lake.

BUCKHURST. Vigorous neyron-rose flowers.

BURGUNDY. Sensational wine-red base, overlaid sheen of velvety black.

CAPRICE. The most outstanding variety of recent years. Strong growing; with striking clusters of deep rose-red.

CARISBROOKE. A.M., R.H.S., 1952 trials. The most popular variety of this section. Huge rose-pink flowers, frilled, with deep maroon blotch. The best known of all the Regals.

CARMINE. A.M., R.H.S. Pure carmine-pink. A really fine flower.

CARNIVAL. A large flowered cerise-red flower on a compact plant.

CAROLE. Rose-Bengal flowers carred above the pale green foliage.

CHORUS GIRL. Deep rose-pink shading to bluish-pink at the throat, very striking.

CONSOLE. Lavender, blotched mahogany, lower petals rose-pink.

COPPER FLAIR. A compact variety. Large pink flower head, copper zoning on leaves.

COUNTESS OF FEVERSHAM. Introduced 1962. Large flowers after the style of 'Quakeress', the colour is soft carmine-rose, each petal flared maroon.

DOREEN FEATHERBY. Large velvety purple flowers almost black. Lighter shading to edge of petals. Very fine.

DORIS FRITH. White flowers with bright amaranth markings.

DUBONNET. Superb wine-red flowers, flushed and overlaid with ,a smoky brown tint.

ELENA BENNET. Rose-pink shading to carmine, overlaid creamy white.

EMMANUEL LIAS. A re-introduction of an old popular variety. Veined shrimp-pink on a softer pink ground.

ENID BLACKABY. A.M., R.H.S. Bright shining orange-crimson, overlaid tile-red.

ETHEL E. KEEN. Creamy-white, with minute soft mauve markings.

FANNY EDEN. Small orange-pink flowers on a white ground quite unique.

FIRE DRAGON. Sparkling signal-red double flowers.

GEORGIA PEACH. Raised by the famous W. Schmidt of the U.S.A. A most striking variety, in a distinctive shade of pink, with frilly petals and a short bushy plant, very self branching. It can be grown either indoors as a pot plant or in an open flower bed. In a reasonable summer a well grown plant

THE REMBRANDT COLLECTION, 5 VAR.

Lucy Leslie   *Circus Day*

Grandma Fischer

82 *Carol*   *Easter Greetings*

THE VANDYKE COLLECTION, 5 VAR.

Barcelona

Parisiana

All My Love

Sienna

Autumn Haze

83

can be expected to develop well over a hundred flower heads in a constant succession of bloom. Full sunlight is essential for bud production. In good light and with a minimum temperature of 50 deg. F., it will flower for months.

GOLDEN PRINCESS. A fine fancy leaved Regal with gold and green foliage. Of dwarf compact habit, it produces white frilly flowers.

GRANDEUR. Large brick-red flowers with bold blotch to each petal.

GRAND SLAM. A.M., R.H.S., awarded Sander Medal, 1956. Large rosy-red flowers, shading to crimson, upper petals violet-red.

GRANDMA FISCHER. A.M., R.H.S. Superb salmon-orange, with brown-black blotch on each petal.

HARVEST MOON. Salmon-apricot, with dark blotch to upper petals.

HOWARDS ORANGE. A.M., 1960. One of the best of the newest orange shades; black flare to most petals.

JOAN FAIRMAN. Introduced 1962. Large frilled flowers of a delicate soft flesh-pink, upper petals shaded maroon.

KATHLEEN EDWARDS. Bold creamy-pink flowers overlaid maroon.

KING MIDAS. Compact plant, orange-red shading to apricot.

LADY IRENE BURTON. A pleasing shade of almost orange-pink with bold maroon blotch. Flowers lightly held against the deep green foliage.

LADY MARY BARING. Large delicate flowers of a soft neyron-rose shade.

LAVENDER CARNIVAL, syn. 'Hilda Jefford'. Large lavender-blue.

LAVENDER GRAND SLAM. Exquisite silvery-mauve sport of that outstanding variety.

LILAC DOMINO. A Carisbrooke seedling, but rather more mauve than pink.

LORD BUTE or PURPLE ROBE. One of the most striking in this section. Small exquisitely edged flowers, deepest velvety purple with intense carmine edge.

MADAME THIRBAUT. Of French origin, this has bright rose-pink splashes on the white petals.

MANX MAID. Charming dwarf type covered with dainty chocolate-maroon flowers.

MARIE ROBER. Superb lavender-violet with deep black staining on each petal.

MARILYN. Huge azalea-pink blossoms. Plant grows rather slowly for the type.

MODIGLIANI. Introduced 1961. A lovely soft orchid-mauve, deeply over-laid violet. An outstanding addition to the colour range.

MRS. E. ANDERSON. Rich azalea-magenta. One of the best regals.

MRS. INNES ROGERS. Rich rose-carmine, fine maroon blotch to upper petals.

MURIEL HARRIS. F.C.C., R.H.S. Lovely pure white, with amethyst pencilling on the upper petals.

MURIEL HAWKINS. Outstandingly large soft pink flowers, frilled and deepening to the edges.

NANCY, LADY ASTOR. C.H. Cattleya-mauve shading to lavender, finely ruffled.

NOCHE. Maroon-red shading to coral-red at the edge of the petals.

PATRICIA COATES. A.M., R.H.S. Compact plant with glowing scarlet-cerise blossoms.

PHYLLIS RICHARDSON. (New). The first double regal pelargonium. Lovely pure pink.

Regal Pelargoniums

PRINCE JOHN, also known as 'Nubian'. This old, well-known variety is a combination of rich crimson and carmine splash to the upper petals.

PRINCESS OF WALES. Glowing strawberry-pink, curiously frilled as to suggest doubleness. A most outstanding plant.

PURPLE ROSE, see 'Lord Bute'.

QUAKERESS, see 'San Diego'.

QUEEN HERMIONE. White base, maroon splash on upper petals.

RAY KELLOGG. Large, pale pink, flushed strawberry.

RHAPSODY. Large, velvety crimson, slight tinge of orange-red.

RHODOMINE. Large rhododendron-like flowers of a delicate mauve with white throat.

ROGUE. Magnificent mahogany-crimson flowers, shading to black on a compact plant, superb addition to the regal type.

SAN DIEGO or QUAKERESS. This originated in the U.S.A. and is a splendid introduction. Rich orchid-mauve flowers with bold purple splash make it a very showy plant.

SENORITA. Vivid salmon-red, reddish-brown stain to upper petals.

TURTLE'S WHITE. A very old variety, but possibly the purest white available of very beautiful form.

VIOLETTA. Small, free flowered type of an unusual violet-blue shading.

VIRTUE. Deep mahogany-red shading to purple.

New varieties of *Pelargonium domesticum* or regal Pelargoniums are regularly being introduced, particularly from the United States. The colour range is truly magnificent, including many striking orange and black shades. Including the following:

ALL MY LOVE. Orchid-mauve and white.

CEZANNE. Purple upper petals, lavender ground.

COVER GIRL. Soft pink, rose shading on upper petals, white throat.

FIRE DANCER. Superb crimson, overlaid dazzling scarlet-maroon.

F. M. MACKENSEN. Clear rose-pink.

GAY NINETIES. White with crimson-rose blotch.

HOUSE AND GARDEN. Scarlet-maroon.

LA PALOMA. White and amaranth.

RED VELVET. Deep burgundy-red, veined and edged crimson and black.

SALMON SPLENDOUR. Apricot-orange, shading to pink with age.

VALENTINE GIRL. Shell-pink, orange-red spot on most petals.

WALLACE FAIRMAN. Wine-red, shading to purple.

WHITE SWAN. Ice-white flowers, some flowers slightly carmine.

WOLFGANG VON GOETHE. Deep red, violet-black mark on petals.

ZULU KING. Upper petals brown-black, suffused rosy red in centre.

There are a number of dwarf forms of *Pelargonium domesticum*, mostly of American origin, among which are the following:

BABY BREEN, of compact habit, the flowers being a blend of lilac and velvety purple.

BABY SNOOKS. This is a small grower, the lavender flowers having lower petals of orchid pink, while there are rosy-violet veins and some red markings.

85

CHICKADEE, is another pleasing variety of dwarf growth, the lavender coloured flowers having a deep violet blotch on the upper petals with smaller markings on the lower petals.

EARLIANA is a dwarf bushy grower, the small flowers having upper petals of maroon colour and the remaining petals being rose-pink with white veinings.

LITTLE RASCAL is similar to 'Earliana', excepting that the upper petals are veined maroon-black, while there are shadings of rosy lilac. The lower petals are of a lighter shade.

MADAME LAYAL is of French origin. This variety is often known as the 'Pansy-flowered Pelargonium'. It makes bushy plants, the flowers having upper petals of dark violet-purple, passing to rose and white, the lower petals being shaded and veined light violet-rose on white ground.

Margot Regal Pelargoniums

One of the most active pelargonium nurseries in Australia is Morfs' 'Margot' Nurseries and their seedlings have won premier awards for a number of years. These include the following all of which have been raised within the in the last six years, being distributed in this country by Mr. K. Hudson.

BLUE BIRD. Huge florets of blue-mauve with a silver sheen.

CAPRICORN. Large, ruffled flesh-pink blooms, top petals veined tan.

CARMINE JOY. Large carmine flowers, waved petals, shading to white throat.

ED BOTH. Ruffled blooms of salmon-rose. Top petals marked chestnut-purple.

EL TORO. Cardinal-red with bronze sheen, and black blotch, waved petals.

FUNNY GIRL. Top petals maroon, lower petals deep rose, white throat.

FLAMENCO. Large rose-madder flowers, crimson blotch. Grey-green foliage.

GEMINI. Flesh-pink shading to white throat. Top petals veined crimson. Ruffled.

GOLD LACE. Golden orange with apricot reverse to petals. Top petals feathered dark red. Enormous trusses on a compact plant.

ISADORA. Deep orchid-pink with red feathering in throat. Extremely ruffled flowers.

JOAN MORF. Basically a white flower but all petals shaded rose-pink. Delicately ruffled and extremely compact. Outstanding.

MORFS' SUMMER STORM. Striking two-tone purple blooms.

MRS. G. MORF. Extremely large clusters of waved persian-rose overlaid magenta, lighter throat. Continuous blooming.

PICADOR. Pleasing blooms of wine red, small chestnut blotches on top petals.

PINK CHIFFON. Heavily ruffled soft pink. Top petals strawberry blotches. An excellent low growing plant.

ROYAL ESCORT. Large flowers of pale pink, shading to white. Top petals feathered purple, small orange blotch.

SUNSET. Pale salmon, with brown blotch and feathering.

TAURUS. Large pink overlaid crimson, strong grower.

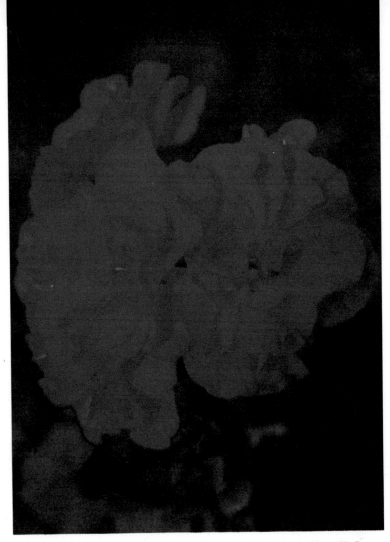

Ivy-leafed Geranium Beryl Wood   *Photo H. Bagust*

9 Ivy-leafed varieties

THE SO-CALLED Ivy-leaved geraniums were, like the Zonals, once extremely popular and widely used for window-boxes, hanging baskets and ornamental vases as well as for making attractive displays in beds and borders when associated with other bedding plants, where their habit of growth enables them to cover a good deal of ground. They can also be used as upright specimens, being tied to light supports and grown against walls or fences or even in the open, when the supports keep the growths erect.

87

It is however, I think, a mistake to refer to this section as climbers, since they have no tendrils or other means of keeping themselves upright. Without support they will always grow horizontally although they do look attractive when trained on light trellis work. This is what makes them so valuable for trailing over ornamental vases and other containers, especially those raised to a good height.

The Ivy-leaved sorts will withstand a good measure of rough treatment – even neglect and poor soil – and yet give a good display of colour. Also, when it is necessary to restrict the growth of the stems, the plants do not object to their growing points being pinched out regularly; in fact the leaves then assume a clean-looking, glossy, dark green colour, and maintain a good shape.

It is possible to build up standard plants by training the main growth and removing all the lateral shoots. Plants thus secured can be grown on for several years with great success. In warm parts of France, Spain and North Africa it is possible to see good healthy specimens growing several feet in height. In Britain, it pays to take a supply of cuttings annually and so have a regular flow of young plants coming to maturity.

In origin, this class of pelargonium descends from the two species *P. peltatum* and *P. hederaefolium*. The stems of this section are thinner, harder and longer jointed than the zonals. Another difference is that whereas the latter will keep on throwing flower spikes in rapid succession, the ivy-leaved sorts seem to produce a lot of bloom at one time, when the plants are literally covered with colour, and then have a short rest, afterwards producing another great profusion of flower heads.

The normal flowering season is from the end of March until October, the plants being bedded out in the open in June and taken under cover again in September, the exact time depending upon the season. Even when out of flower, the plants remain ornamental on account of their glossy green, attractively shaped leaves. While they will sometimes flower during the winter, they cannot be depended on at all for this purpose.

Varieties as always, must be a matter of personal choice, and although few of the really older sorts are now available, those which are still in cultivation remain as reliable as they ever were and, with some of the newer varieties, make it possible to secure a very wide range of desirable colours. As far as I am aware, the only variegated ivy-leaved geranium obtainable today is the variety 'L'Eleganté' which is the survivor of a small section of coloured-leaved ivies. The white edging to the dark green, shapely leaves, gives the plant a striking appearance and makes it most outstanding, whether grown singly or grouped with other sorts.

If the plants are put outdoors during the summer and are kept in a low temperature, the leaves have a tendency to assume a violet-mauve hue, and it is sometimes asserted that the leaves emit a faint but pleasant perfume if they are rubbed or bruised. The whitish flowers are often shaded blush and feathered with reddish-purple markings.

While the number of named varieties of Ivy-leaved geraniums in cultivation is not nearly so large as that of the zonals, there are literally scores of first-class varieties available in a wide colour range. They have the added distinction, in nearly all cases, of having brighter coloured veinings and often featherings and other markings on the petals.

The following is a list of some of the better named varieties:

ABEL CARRIERE. Double, orchid-purple.

ALICE CROUSSE. Double, free flowering magenta.

ACHIEVEMENT. Vigorous growing, with large clusters of semi-double, soft cerise pink.

ADMIRAL BYRD. Semi-double, lilac-pink with cerise markings.

ALBA PLENA. Semi-double, pure white, of American origin.

BRIDESMAID. Large double, soft orchid-pink, the upper petals being veined and marked red.

BUTTERFLIES. A single of unusual colouring, cyclamen-purple with reddish markings.

CAPRICE. Semi-double, silvery pink. Upper petals marked crimson.

CHARLES TURNER. *See* 'Souvenir de Charles Turner'.

COLONEL BADEN-POWELL. Semi-double, white, flushed deep lavender, blotched and feathered purple-cerise.

CROCODILE. Pink flowers. The medium green foliage has veins which are picked out in white or cream.

EMILY SYLVIA. Large semi-double, silvery rose-pink.

EULALIA. Fully double and very lovely, the rosette flowers being deep blue-mauve; this is sometimes known as 'Blue Peter'.

FRED A. BODE. Large semi-double red flowers with maroon feathering.

GALILEE. One of the best known of all Ivy-leaved geraniums. A great favourite for bedding and window-boxes, the double rose-pink flowers remaining in good condition for a long time.

JACK OF HEARTS. Soft salmon. A recent introduction from the U.S.A.

JEANNE D'ARC. Of dwarf habit, the mauvish-white flowers being veined carmine.

JESTER. Large double, orchid-pink, flecked rose-pink.

LA FRANCE. Freely produced lilac flowers feathered maroon.

LAVENDER GEM. Double, pale lavender flowers with dark green leaves. Of dwarf habit.

L'ELEGANTÉ. Leaves of good shape, variegated with cream and purple and distinctly scented. The small single flowers are white with reddish-purple featherings often giving the appearance of being very pale pink. These flowers are very freely produced. It has been in cultivation for well over a century.

LEOPARD. Semi-double, orchid-pink, spotted and veined cerise.

LUCKY STRIKE. Medium sized flowers, deep rose-pink or tyrian rose, the upper petals being blotched and feathered a deeper shade.

MRS. MARTIN. Dwarf growing, double flowers of soft pale mauve.

MRS. BANKS. Blush-white, upper petals marked light violet.

MRS. H. J. JONES. A very old variety developed at the Ryecroft Nurseries of H. J. Jones at the beginning of the century. The double deep rose-pink flowers are shaded with salmon.

MRS. W A. R. CLIFTON Large vigorous habit, orient-red, central petals sometimes white on reverse.

OLD MEXICO. Semi-double, the large clusters of flowers being of bright rose-cerise with slight violet undercurrent.

PRINCESS VICTORIA. Synonymous with 'La France' and 'Enchantress'.

DR. CHIPAULT. Large bright red, shaded cerise. Excellent for cutting.

QUEEN OF HEARTS. White with scarlet heart shaped markings on each petal.

90   *Ivy-leafed Pelargonium Balcon Rouge*   *Photo H. Smith*

Ivy-leafed Pelargonium Mme. Crousse   *Photo H. Smith*

RYECROFT SURPRISE. A double salmon-pink of really good habit.

SANTA PAULA. Double flowers of rich lavender.

SIR PERCY BLAKENEY. A first-class variety with good sized, showy, geranium-lake flowers.

SIR A. HORT. Of vigorous slender habit, pink with red markings.

SNOWDRIFT or DOUBLE WHITE. Has medium sized, double white flowers with slight blush shadings at the base of the petals.

SOUVENIR DE CHARLES TURNER. Although old, still one of the best; double rose-pink.

Hybrid Ivy-leaved Pelargoniums

These have come from *P. peltatum* crossed with *P. hortorum*. Although there are many Ivy-leaved geraniums which have been influenced by zonal

91

antecedents, the following clearly display the influence of the two parents more than many of the other sorts:

JAMES T. HARRISON. This has rather a straggly habit with the typical slender, brittle stems of the Ivy-leaved varieties, although the foliage and flowers are somewhat like those of the zonal type. The semi-double flowers are orient-red.

LADY GERTRUDE. A semi-double variety of which the purple upper petals have a base of white and there is a purplish blotch.

LULLABY. The erect stems bear medium sized flowers of double salmon-apricot.

MADAM CHARMET. Semi-double flowers of soft scarlet, with a medium zonal habit.

MILKY WAY. Of dwarf zonal habit, the semi-double, medium sized flowers of an off-white colour being typically those of the Ivy geranium.

MILLFIELD GEM. One of the best of all hybrid Ivies, the semi-double medium sized flowers being amaranth-rose blotched and feathered a rosy red. This variety is also known as 'Victory'.

MRS. HAMILTON. Semi-double, smallish flowers of signal-red flushed vermilion.

MRS. JOHN DAY. Medium sized semi-double flowers of bright crimson.

RAMONA. Large double, vermilion-red and rose. A pleasing variety of which some of the stems grow almost upright, others being quite lax as is the case with typical Ivy-leaved varieties.

10 Variegated-leafed Geraniums

IT IS NOT only on account of their flowers that zonal pelargoniums are so attractive, for many of them have showy foliage, the leaves being prettily coloured and marked. At various times they have been described as 'show off' geraniums, 'the painted-leaved cranes bills' and 'striped-leaved' geraniums. Certainly there have been coloured-leaved varieties in cultivation for nearly 250 years.

It was not until about 1853, however, that this type of geranium had any real interest taken in it. Then Peter Grieve, gardener of Culford Hall, Bury St. Edmunds, became keenly interested in these plants and over the space of fifteen or sixteen years, he investigated, improved and brought into being a number of coloured-leaved varieties including those known as the golden-tricolours. This man's name has been made famous in the geranium world by his book on the variegated varieties, although this volume has been out of print for many years.

Fortunately the British Geranium Society have issued this book in parts, with its quarterly bulletins, so that there is now freely available the information as set down by Grieve. Writing about 120 years ago, Grieve said, 'Variegation in the foliage of plants may be justly considered as an interesting phenomenon and present knowledge of the subject furnishes us with no information whatever with its cause or causes. Hence we are unacquainted with certain means of producing it. It has always been considered by some intelligent persons, as analogous to disease and it is quite certain that its presence is generally, if not always, accompanied by a considerable amount of debility or at least by a diminution of constitutional vigour, which in some degree, furnishes argument in support of this view of its nature. It would appear that there are very few if any, orders or families in the vegetable kingdom, in which it does not occasionally appear, from the oaks, the elms etc., of our woods and forests, to the chickweed which infests our gardens and cultivated grounds. Scientific men do not appear as yet to have given this subject a great amount of attention and it would, of course, be like presumption on my part to attempt to offer anything like an elucidation of a matter so mysterious and important. I may however, be allowed to say that the subject appears to me to offer a very wide and interesting field for scientific inquiry and research.'

Grieve then goes on to mention what happens in regard to other plants or shrubs with variegated leaves and instances experiments with leaves showing

Pelargonium Golden Harry Hieover   *Photo H. Smith*

that they had cells filled with air or gas in immediate contact with the chloro-phyll or colouring substance. The parts of the leaves which were green, had no such cells filled with gas in contact with the chlorophyll. This would seem to indicate that the chlorophyll is neutralized or rendered colourless by the immediate contact or presence of these air cells. Whether this is really so or not, it is believed that the leaves of plants are the natural appendages of the branches and are in fact an extension or continuation of the rind of the stem and branches. The thin transparent skin with which the leaf is covered is also an extension of the epidermis or outer skin of the plants.

Variegation shows itself in a variety of forms, for example in the case of the shrub *Aucuba japonica*, the entire leaf is spotted or blotched, whilst with *Lonicera aureo-reticulata* the surface of the leaves is beautifully reticulated. Other plants have irregular spots of yellow and of other colours. With pelargoniums however, although plants in their early stages of growth, par-ticularly those from seeds, produce leaves with irregular spots or blotches, as the plant grows older, these resolve themselves into some regular form of marginal variegation. It was assumed by Grieve, as by other experts since, that double flowers and variegated foliage are incompatible with each other in the same individual plant. This is because, it is said, that doubleness of

94

Variegated-leafed Geraniums

flowers is an indication of strength whilst variegated foliage is probably some kind of weakness. This, of course, is not a hundred per cent true, since there are some instances of plants with double flowers having variegated foliage.

Whilst it may perhaps be true that variegated foliage is something separate from coloured foliage, as far as the coloured-leaved geraniums are concerned we will consider them together. An ordinary variegated leaf found on many types of plants may very well be due to a deficiency of some kind, whereas actual coloration of the leaves is probably due to something being added to the green.

It is not possible to say for certain how colour variations first arose, since in the earliest known pelargoniums, variegated forms were unknown. It seems certain that originally at least, the coloured-leaved forms came about as a result of chlorophyll deficiency. Some nurserymen were quick to see that the unusualness of the coloured leaves would make the plants of extra value and they therefore set to work to raise more varieties. So great was their success that today, there are sorts not only with light green and yellow markings, but others having leaves marked or veined with cream and silver, gold, bronze, brown and purple.

Pelargonium Caroline Schmidt   *Photo H. Smith*

For the most part flowers of the coloured foliaged sorts are rather small, although 'Mrs. Parker', which is described later, has a really good-sized truss. Since it is for their foliage that these plants are grown, blooms are not of the first importance. The bicolour or tricolour leaves are remarkably blended, and whether kept in the greenhouse all the year or bedded out in the summer, they are most effective, as everyone who has seen them used at Kew Gardens or at Wisley or the larger parks, will agree.

In addition, now that house plants are rapidly gaining in popularity, the wide choice of colour available in variegated geraniums makes them high on the list of 'no trouble' indoor plants, providing an interesting show for a long period, coupled with an air of old-fashioned romance.

It is true to say that in common with most variegated plants, the fancy-leaved geraniums are just a little more difficult to grow than the green foliaged sorts and those which show the brightest colours are perhaps slightly weaker in constitution, although this may also be due to the rather smaller root system they make. In any case it is essential, for the finest results, to provide really sharp drainage and where plants are permanently kept in pots, the receptacles should not be too large, otherwise too much growth may be made, which often spoils the shape of a plant.

Another important point is that since the leaves of this type of geranium are rather thick and yet soft, they are inclined to rot off if kept in an atmosphere which is too close and humid. Since it is the newest shoots which are the most colourful, it pays to encourage fresh growth and so enjoy the full benefit of the brightest shades. When a plant is inclined to become leggy, the growing centre can either be cut back and made into a cutting and potted up, or just be pinched back in the usual way. In either case, fresh growth will be stimulated by the stopping of the taller stems. A winter temperature of around 60 deg. F. will help to maintain the plants in good healthy condition and a period in the open during the summer leads to healthier, stronger plants.

Apart from being grown in pots and borders by themselves, they may be used to advantage in combination with the ordinary bedding zonal sorts, and in this connection, it is quite in order and sometimes advisable, to remove the flowers before they open, so that attention becomes focused on the foliage itself.

Before mentioning some of the best varieties of the ornamental-leaved sorts there is a little group of bicoloured varieties known as the 'Butterfly' geraniums because of the leaf markings, which resemble a butterfly in flight. The two best known varieties are: 'Crystal Palace Gem' with yellowish-green leaves, an irregular central blotch, and small single bright scarlet flowers, and 'A Happy Thought', a smaller sort, the margin of the leaves being green, the central markings yellow. It has striking magenta flowers. Like most of the fancy varieties, they do not make really large specimens, and the leaves remain on the small side, always a characteristic of the Butterfly geraniums.

For easy reference the Fancies may be divided into separate colour sections. Although there are so many named sorts still available, only a selection can be mentioned because of lack of space.

Of the Silver-leaved varieties, 'Flower of Spring', a strong growing sort, has been known for nearly one hundred years. It is still one of the very best of its colour, with an unusually wide, irregular deep ivory border. It carries small single scarlet flowers. 'Caroline Schmidt' has a border of straw-yellow and is unusual for the large size of its deep cerise flowers and the rather ruffled edges of its leaves.

'Chelsea Gem' is another good sort and appears to be identical with 'Mrs.' or 'Lady Churchill'. The plants are short-jointed with tall shell-pink flowers. 'Mrs. Mapping' is similar to 'Flower of Spring' excepting that the flowers are white with a pink shading in the centre. 'Mrs. Parker' is a double rose-pink and one of the finest of all the silver-leaved sorts being much used for bedding.

'Madame Salleron' is a really old variety, sometimes known as 'Dandy'. It is very dwarf growing forming a compact bush of no more than 4 or 5 inches high and is therefore ideal for bedding or as an edging variety. This unusual habit of growth leads to really bushy plants which as far as is known, do not produce any flowers at all; quite an unusual characteristic for any kind of pelargonium. It makes a splendid contrast when planted with other dwarf growing sorts especially those which have foliage with darker zonings, since the foliage is a glossy silver-green. In old catalogues this variety was sometimes listed as 'Little Dorrit'–quite appropriately named. Another old variety similar to 'Madame Salleron' (of which it is considered to be a sport) is 'Little Trot', which has rather quaint small, single pink flowers with an attractive silver colouring in the leaves. Included in this section too, are the two scented-leaved sorts *Pelargonium crispum variegatum* and 'Lady Plymouth', referred to on pages 99 and 100.

Of the golden-leaved sorts, in addition to 'A Happy Thought' and 'Crystal Palace Gem' already mentioned, there are a number of others worthy of consideration and well worth hunting for. 'Golden Crampel' is a dwarf with the absence of any zone or markings in the leaves, which no doubt is the reason of its sometimes being known as the 'Golden Leaf Geranium'. Its single red flowers, which are freely produced, have a showy white eye. 'Verona' is somewhat similar, although the flowers are pinky-magenta.

There are also some excellent tricolour-leaved sorts and 'Mrs. Henry Cox' is one of the most widely used. It has really brilliant-hued foliage which, in addition to the gold colour, contains red, purple and other shades, going on to an almost black shade; a dwarf grower it produces salmon-pink flowers. 'Mrs. Pollock' too, finds many admirers, and is largely used in formal beds laid out by public authorities. The flat, deeply serrated leaves are marked with pale gold, purple and red, the colour of the flowers being scarlet-vermilion.

Very similar is 'Mrs. Strang', although in this case, the flowers are double cerise and the foliage seems to be particularly bright and showy. 'Golden Harry Hieover', is a splendid free growing dwarf, golden-leaved and bronzy-red zoned, making a compact yet bushy plant, of no more than 5 inches in height. Producing constant supplies of vermilion-scarlet flowers, it is particularly suitable for edging purposes.

Another interesting variety which commands attention is 'Lass O' Gowrie'. It has single vermilion flowers and leaves of yellow, irregularly zoned reddish-purple and green.

Of the plants on which the leaves have a bronzy zone, 'Marechal McMahon' is probably the best known, its single red flowers being carried on rather thin stems. These however, are often removed before they open without any loss of display, since the colouring of the leaves is most showy, taking in, apart from the bronze, shades of green, gold, bright and deep red, the actual bronze zone itself being more prominent as the foliage fully develops.

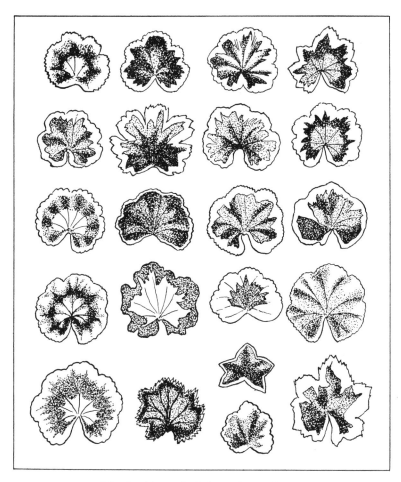

Fig. 4. Fancy-leafed zonal geraniums

A silver-leaved tricolour of high merit is 'Miss Burdett Coutts', of which the foliage has shadings of pink and purple on a creamy-yellow base. It is a slow grower, and not very easy to propagate, which is probably the reason it is so expensive to buy at the present time. 'Mrs. Quilter' is a vigorous grower, with well zoned reddish-chestnut, yellowish-green leaves, the single flowers being shell-pink.

An American variety, 'Skies of Italy', is a very attractive tricolour, having deeply toothed leaves, with yellow edges and zoned with crimson-orange. Here again, the single flowers are of a vermilion colour. 'Bronze Queen' too, is another popular variety with fairly large leaves which have a prominent chestnut zone. The single flowers are rich Indian-lake.

A very famous old variety is 'Red Black Vesuvius', which is really a miniature growing sort, having nearly black leaves with just a trace of green evident. The

98

Variegated-leafed Geraniums

trusses of showy scarlet flowers are carried nicely above the foliage, and so provide a pleasing contrast to the colour of the leaves. There is a form known as 'Salmon Black Vesuvius' which is similar in leaf and habit to the previously mentioned sort but the flowers are of a showy salmon colour.

Yet another similar variety is 'Mephistopheles' which is even more heavily zoned black, and rather stronger growing than 'Red Black Vesuvius'. Quite different is 'Black Douglas', an altogether brighter variety, the gold-coloured leaves having a wide bronze zone. It makes good growth and produces single salmon-pink flowers. Another unusual sort is 'Distinction', or 'One in a Ring', which has lively green foliage and a sharply divided black zone forming a picotée edge to each leaf. The zone or ring being nearer the edge than is usual. The plant is of dwarf habit and carries red flowers which show up well.

A variety which is unusual in another way is 'Mrs. G. Clark', since it not only has pale green leaves but particularly white stems, which is a characteristic of another little known sort, 'Turtle's Surprise'.

If only one could refer to catalogues issued early this century, it is certain that many more most interesting coloured foliaged varieties would be found fully described. Even so, although this is not possible, it is surprising how many of the really old sorts have survived, which is an indication of their real worth. Their survival is surely an indication that they refuse to be ousted by new creations, however good and attractive the latter may be.

Some of the very best of the old sorts may even now be growing on remote cottage window-sills, or in conservatories where old-fashioned subjects are valued and where they await our discovery.

Fragrans Variegata   *Photo F. G. Read*

Although by no means a complete list, the following varieties are among the very best of the variegated varieties. Some may need a little searching for, but the possession of any of them will be rewarding.

Ornamental or Variegated-leaved varieties

ADAM'S QUILT. A bright golden bicolour, single rose-pink flowers.

A FREAK OF NATURE. A curious plant with almost pure white stems and conspicuous white butterfly in the centre of each leaf.

A HAPPY THOUGHT. One of the best. Bold creamy-yellow butterfly in the centre of each leaf. Striking magenta flowers.

BEAUTY OF CALDERDALE. Rich chocolate zone on clear emerald-green leaf. Single scarlet flowers.

BETH WATTS. Pale golden leaf and soft porcelain-rose, single flowers.

BLAKESDORF. Charming almost black-leafed miniature, with primitive orange-red single flowers.

BRONZE CORINNE. Free growing, golden leaves with double, scarlet flowers.

BRONZE QUEEN. Strong golden leaves with clear chestnut zone. Large Indian-lake flowers.

CAROLINE SCHMIDT. One of the finest bedding geraniums. The bold double scarlet flowers stand out against the white variegated foliage.

CHELSEA GEM, syn. 'Lady Churchill'. Silvery white variegated leaves with double shell-pink flowers.

CRAMPEL'S MASTER. Deep olive-green leaves with centre streaked gold. Large scarlet flowers.

CREED'S SEEDLING. Golden leaves with small bright scarlet flowers.

CRYSTAL PALACE GEM. Golden leaf with yellow markings, single red flowers.

DISTINCTION, syn. 'One in a Ring'. Deep olive-green leaf, the black zone forming a picotée edge to the leaf.

DOLLY VARDON. Silver tricolour, most showy.

FLOWER OF THE DAY. Extremely old and rare variety, yellow leaf, bronze zone, single orange-red flower.

FRIESDORF. A miniature dwarf growing. Almost black-green leaf with bright orange-red primitive flowers.

GOLDEN CREST. A new introduction 1960. A beautifully crimped greeny-golden leaf, with distinct salmon-pink flowers.

GOLDEN HARRY HIEOVER. Golden-leaved dwarf variety. Bright scarlet flowers.

GOLDEN ORFE. A wonderful new variety, zoned lettuce-green to gold leaf, huge goldfish-pink single flowers.

HARRISON WEIR. Strong clear chocolate zone on yellow ground. Clear pink, single flowers.

HIDCOTE CRIMSON. Golden leaves with rich chestnut zone, deep crimson flowers.

HIS MAJESTY, syn. 'The Czar'. A true stock of this old favourite has a very large chocolate zone, orange-red single flowers.

KATHLEEN HARROP. A true strain of this variety. Begonia-lake flowers on white and green foliage.

LASS O' GOWRIE. A silver tricolour with scarlet flowers.

MADAM BUTTERFLY. White leaves, green butterfly markings, double deep crimson flowers.

MADAME SALLERON. Small variegated non-flowering variety for edging.

MANGLES VARIEGATED, syn. 'Manglesi'. Of semi-prostrate form. Greenish-yellow leaf with green butterfly markings, intense orange-red single flowers.

MAGENTA MACMAHON. Lesser bronze zone than parent, bright single magenta flowers.

MARECHAL MACMAHON. Rich brown zone, large single orange-red flowers, slight white eye.

MASTERPIECE. Double rose-pink flowers on bronze foliage.

MISS BURDETT COUTTS. The most outstanding tricolour. The variegations of colour on a creamy yellow base make this a great treasure.

MOUNTAINS OF SNOW. Outstanding variety, white edging to leaf, flowers almost rose-pink.

MRS. HENRY COX. The most brilliant of tricolours, including bronze, red and creamy yellow variegations.

MRS. MAPPIN. Strong silver-leaved type, with almost white flowers.

MRS. PARKER. Fine white variegation, with striking rose-pink blossoms.

MRS. POLLOCK. Well-known golden-leaved variety, with bronze zone.

MRS. QUILTER. Bright shell-pink single flowers, on vigorous bronze foliage.

PINK HAPPY THOUGHT. Pale green leaf, yellow butterfly markings, with bright pink single flowers.

ROBERT FISH. A very rare old variety for edging, full golden leaves, bright begonia-red flowers.

VERONA. Golden, lettuce-green leaves, with bright pink flowers.

Many of the once widely grown ornamental-leaved pelargoniums no longer appear to be in cultivation, but whenever they can be found, they are well worth securing. Among the difficult to find sorts are the following, which were once mentioned by Peter Grieve and other writers of the last century:

Golden variegated varieties

LUCY GRIEVE. One of the most beautiful tricolour-leaved varieties, exquisitely figured by a brilliant surface-zone of lake-tinted crimson upon an under bronze ground, with very rich golden margins; excellent for winter decoration and also as a bedding plant.

SOPHIA CUSAK. A beautiful and very effective variety, with bright-flamed scarlet zone, upon a broken bronze border, bright golden-yellow margins; making a fine compact pot plant, useful for winter decoration and as a bedding plant.

SOPHIA DUMARESQUE. A fine, robust, and vigorous variety, freely branched with rich golden-margined foliage, effectively marked by a brilliant flame-tinted zone; a very fine bedding plant, excellent for winter decoration.

SPANISH BEAUTY. A dwarf-growing variety, broad pure lemon-yellow margins well defined, dark bronze leaf zone, overlaid with a bright-flamed scarlet tint; a very picturesque and effective variety.

FAIRY SPELL. A beautiful and very effective dwarf-branching variety, with well-expanded leaves of circular outline; the green disc belted with a bronze zone finely marked and barred with carmine-scarlet upon a broad rich canary-yellow leaf margin.

101

HUMMING BIRD. In the style of 'Lady Cullum', with sub-erect robust growth and evenly expanded leaves of good substance, marked by a broad metallic zone of bronze margined with rich flamed crimson in summer; picturesque and distinct in character by its violet-rose tints during the winter months.

COUNTESS OF CRAVEN. An even and well-defined broad margin of clear golden-yellow, with rich crimson and bronze zone; habit compact and vigorous.

SUNRAY. Leaves of good substance, somewhat convex; broad dark brown zone, barred with deep red; small disc of bright green, with narrow margin of bright golden-yellow; close, compact and vigorous in habit; altogether a very fine variety for pot culture and winter decoration, and likely to prove a fine bedding plant.

JETTY LACY. This is a very pretty and much admired variety; leaves neatly margined with rich golden-yellow; broad zone of rich crimson and chestnut-red of vigorous growth and compact habit.

BEAUTY OF SURREY. Margin of leaf rich yellow, with zone of brilliant carmine-red, and dark brown or black; centre small and bright green; a very distinct and novel variety.

MRS. EYRE CRABB. Foliage with a deep or broad margin of bright yellow; conspicuous vandyked zones, richly barred or belted with bright-flamed carmine.

RUSTIC BEAUTY. This is a novel and distinct variety, the flowers being clear white: the habit of the plant is dwarf and compact, leaves roundly lobed, with a light flame-coloured zone, and bright lemon-yellow leaf margins.

RESPLENDENT. Foliage of medium size, flat and nearly circular; zone very broad colour rich brown-red shot with cherry-red, even yellow margin; this is a very fine and very distinct variety.

BEAUTIFUL FOR EVER. One of the most brilliant zoned varieties in its group, of fine form and substance; altogether very effective; bright carmine-scarlet zone of great width, and belted by a proportionately broad bright yellow margin; will prove a grand competition plant, and excellent for winter decoration.

PETER GRIEVE. A robust-growing variety of excellent habit, with slightly convex, smooth, and well-rounded leaves, a vandyked fiery zone, and leaf margins of rich yellow. In point of habit and shape of leaf the introduction of this variety marked a decided advance.

SULTANA VALIDA. A splendid variety, something in the way of the 'Prince of Wales', but with a very bright straw-yellow margin, will also prove a fine exhibition plant.

PLUTARCH. Leaves large, round and smooth; very flat, and of stout leatherly substances; small green centre, with broad black zone, illuminated on outer edge with scarlet-crimson; regular margin of bright yellow; very free growth; hardy and robust.

ROUGE ET NOIR. Leaves of medium size, green centre, with narrow black zone, surrounded with bright red, succeeded by a broad margin of deep yellow.

GLISTENING SEA. A very ornamental variety, with a broad golden-yellow leaf margin and well-defined narrow zone of bright carmine; leaf of good substance and outline habit dwarf and compact.

RETICULATUM. A nosegay variety, with large trusses of rich scarlet flowers, similar to the well-known variety 'Stella'. The foliage shows a dark-shaded

Pelargonium Mme. Salleron   *Photo H. Smith*

zone and the entire surface is marked by a beautiful tracery or network of golden veins upon a green ground.

Silver variegated varieties

ITALIA UNITA. Zone of bright carmine-rose colour; scarlet flowers, with white eye; a very beautiful variety for either pot-culture or as a bedding plant.

SILVER CLOUD. A compact and very free-growing variety, with well-expanded foliage; bronze zone, finely belted and barred with flame-coloured rose; flowers rich scarlet.

CHARMING BRIDE. Robust free habit, with rich bronze zone, barred with bright rose-carmine; flower brilliant rich scarlet, with white eye; fine truss; a splendid bedding variety and a very fine pot plant.

BANSHEE. Margin of leaf rich cream; zone pink-lake; large foliage; free and compact habit of growth; flowers cerise and scarlet; free bloomer, good truss.

PERI. Leaf margin silver-white; foliage large, with good-sized zone of bright lake; habit of plant strong; free, and compact; a very bright and lively variety.

LA VESTALE. Delicate creamy-white margin; zone lake-pink; light green leaf-centre rendering the plant peculiarly chaste in colour and distinct in character; large scarlet flowers; large truss.

EXCELLENT. A very good habited variety, with highly coloured carmine zone, bright green centre and white margins; was awarded first prize as the best Silver Variegated Zonal at the Special Pelargonium Show at South Kensington, on May 22, 1869.

SILVER CHAIN. Pure white margin, rosy-pink flowers; one of the best silver-margined varieties, being of compact and dwarf habit, ample foliage; well adapted for ribbon-lines, etc.

WALTHAM BRIDE. A fine compact close-habited variety, the flowers rising just above the foliage in good-sized trusses, producing in great abundance, and in colour pure white; centre of leaf dark green with broad white margin.

BRIGHT STAR. A short-jointed robust variety, with broad edge of creamy-white; took first prize in its class at the Special Pelargonium Show at Kensington on May 22, 1869.

Bronze Zonal varieties

COUNTESS OF KELLIE. Leaves bright golden-yellow with light chestnut zone, shaded with bright red; habit vigorous and compact, a fine and effective bedder.

KENTISH HERO. Large leaves of a light greenish-yellow colour, with a broad zone of dark bronze; vigorous grower; a very distinct and striking variety.

CROWN PRINCE. A very handsome variety with a high-coloured chestnut zone.

ST. JOHN'S WOOD STAR. Brilliant red zone upon a yellow leaf-ground with a pure gold outer margin; a very beautiful and effective variety.

FEU DE JOIE. Large leaves, slightly convex, clear golden-yellow with broad zone of cherry-red; habit free and compact; flowers rose-carmine; a very distinct variety.

CRITERION. Rich golden-yellow ground with broad even belt of rich chestnut-red with neat golden margin; foliage very large and rather flat; a very fine variety.

SIBYL. A very distinct and striking variety of dwarf and compact habit; foliage medium size; colour deep chestnut-brown with small circular centre and very narrow even margin of yellow; flowers rich scarlet. One of the finest bedding varieties.

PLUTUS. Rich golden-yellow with chestnut zone of medium depth and well defined.

MRS. ALAN LOWNDES. Yellow leaf-ground with broad chestnut zone; fine foliage and habit. A fine variety.

IMPERATRICE EUGENIE. Leaves very large, irregular surface and ground colour light sulphury yellow with very broad zone of dark bronzy-chocolate, covering nearly two-thirds of the surface of the leaf; a very fine and distinct variety.

11 Scented-leafed Geraniums

FOR HUNDREDS of years the scented-leaved geraniums have been favourites among all classes of people. This is not surprising in view of their ease of culture, and the great variety of the decorative foliage, coupled with the tremendously wide range of scents available. Many of the scented-leaved sorts are species, while a large number of others are varieties which have been raised intentionally, or have come about as natural hybrids. Although there is a considerable difference in the habit of growth, all are easy to cultivate.

Gardeners of a century ago certainly knew the value of fragrance, for not only were these plants used in conservatories and living-rooms, but they were planted alongside garden walls where the leaves could be thumbed and the scents enjoyed. Scented geraniums always make interesting plants for garden beds, tubs, vases, and window-boxes. Another point in their favour is that they will thrive in town gardens and will withstand the most casual treatment, although they readily respond to any little extra attention given.

Obviously, since the plants, with their perfumes, are particularly valuable during the winter, they will appreciate good treatment during the summer, so that during that time, they should have the benefit of all the sun there is, in order to build up plenty of well-ripened growths.

Where plants are kept permanently in pots, it is a good plan to give an occasional feed of liquid manure during the summer, which will make the leaves of really good appearance, and any re-potting necessary, can be carried out either in March or September, using a compost made up of sandy loam, some sifted decayed manure or leaf mould, and a little bone meal, which will provide nourishment over a long period and just as and when required.

As something of a change, the foliage can be used for table decoration, for although the flowers of the scented sorts are not particularly large or decorative, the foliage is definitely ornamental.

Whether grown in the greenhouse, conservatory or when bedded out, the scented geraniums act as a kind of magnet, for they compel the onlooker, including those most uninterested in plant growing, to touch the foliage and thereby obtain a refreshing perfume. Much has been written and said about the loss of scent in the musk, sweet peas and heliotrope but such a charge can never be made concerning the scented-leaved geraniums.

There is no typical variety, for the habit of growth and shape of foliage is very diverse indeed and in all cases the scent is 'held' by the leaves. Once they are lightly pressed or rubbed, they yield their scent, which of course, is the

Fig. 5.   Different forms of scented-leafed geraniums

result of the rubbing or light bruising having forced out the aromatic oils contained in the leaf tissues.

It is sometimes possible to find in the windows of country cottages, really handsome scented-leaved varieties. There is no doubt that this type of geranium is as popular today as it was during the reign of Charles I. It was at that time, 1632 to be exact, that sailors and travellers first brought this particular type of plant from South Africa to England.

It was not, however, until the Victorian period that they came to be grown by the cottager. Until that time they were possessed, mainly, by the wealthy classes. In the pleasure grounds of big houses where social functions were held, it was the custom to have planted along the garden paths during the summer, a variety of scented-leaved pelargoniums so that the leaves could be touched or picked as guests walked through the gardens.

Pelargonium Denticulatum   *Photo F. G. Read*

Although the flowers of the scented-leaved geraniums are not as showy as those in the other groups, in some cases they are certainly attractive, but it is the perfumed foliage which makes the plants so appealing.

It is difficult to group these varieties either in regard to their leaf pattern or their scent. Fortunately, most of them are easily cultivated and they will prove to be a delight whether they are grown in a pot in the living-room or greenhouse, or used as garden plants during the summer.

It is said that there are over 200 species and varieties of scented geraniums. Some bring the fragrance of fruit such as lime, lemon, strawberry and apple. Some are spice-scented, reminding one of nutmeg, ginger or pepper; quite a number have a delightful rose perfume and one or two emit a strong, almost heady smell. It must also be said that the scent of a few varieties is far from attractive.

One difficulty in regard to grouping the perfumed-leaved sorts is that some cross-pollinate and seed freely. In one or two instances, notably with *Pelargonium graveolens,* this has resulted in an abundance of offspring, many of which are very similar to named varieties already in cultivation.

Some are dwarf growing, others such as 'Clorinda', are quite large; some   107 have quite small leaves while others have really large foliage. One or two species such as *P. fragrans,* have almost entire leaves while other are very finely cut.

It would be quite impossible to include all the varieties here, even if they were known. The following are among the very best sorts and are grouped under their main scents, although at times, one discovers that individual plants appear to have more than one scent, making it difficult to distinguish which is the main one.

Then there are some which are densely hairy, including *P. tomentosum,* while some are without hairs. There are also varieties having variegated as well as the more usual green leaves. Here then, is a section of the great Pelargonium family which is attractive in form, colour, size and perfume. No wonder the scented-leaved geraniums are increasing in popularity.

There are very many species having scented leaves and many of these have also given rise to hybrids, some of which have been named, although many, with different names, are extremely alike, especially the oak-leaved varieties. Some of these are beautifully patterned and it is only when a group of them are seen together, that one realizes the range available and also the similarity of varieties.

Lemon-scented Pelargoniums
P. citriodorum, 'Prince of Orange'. Tall, bushy plants with light green, fan-shaped leaves. Large white flowers tinged with pink. Upper petals veined purple.

P. crispum, 'Prince Rupert'. Strong lemon scent. Large, handsome plant with orchid flowers veined purple.

P. crispum lactifolia. Fruity orange scent. Medium-sized leaves.

P. crispum minor, 'Finger Bowl Geranium'. Tiny, stemless leaves, with strong citronella scent. Pale lavender flowers.

P. limoneum, 'Lady Mary'. Tall grower, fan-shaped, light green leaves. Magenta bloom.

P. mellisimum. Tri-lobed, lemon-scented leaves. A handsome sturdy plant.

P. nervosum, 'Lime Scented'. Deep green lime-scented leaves. Woody stemmed with trailing branches.

Mint-scented Pelargoniums
P. denticulatum tomentosum, 'Pungent Peppermint'. Deeply cut, hairy leaves. Wonderful mint scent. A tall grower.

P. tomentosum, 'Peppermint'. Large grape-like, hairy leaves. Low, spreading growth.

P. tomentosum graveolens, 'Joy Lucile'. Strong mint scent. Large triangularly lobed light green, 'felt' leaves. Pink flowers.

Rose-scented Pelargoniums
P. adcifolium, 'Snowflake Rose'. An extra large plant with mammoth fan-shaped leaves, blotched with white. Lavender blooms.

P. capitatum, 'Attar of Roses'. Tall growing, with deeply cut, highly scented leaves and small orchid flowers.

P. denticulatum, 'Fern Leaf'. The finest cut leaf of all. A tall, spreading plant which resembles some ferns. Tiny white flowers.

P. graveolens camphorum, 'Camphor Rose'. Deeply cut, camphor-scented leaves. The small orchid flowers are purple veined.

P. graveolens giganteum. Sweet rose-scented, large leaves on a spreading plant.

P. graveolens, 'Lady Plymouth'. A strong rose scent. Silvery-grey leaves with white margins.

SHRUBLAND ROSE. Large crinkly leaves with red flowers. Compact bushy plants.

Fruit-scented Pelargoniums

P. fragrans, 'Cody's Nutmeg'. A cross between apple and nutmeg geraniums, with tiny white flowers.

FILBERT. The light green, hairy leaves and stems are nut-scented. Red flowers, veined maroon.

P. odoratissimum, apple-scented. Light green velvety leaves on compact plants. Tiny white flowers, with red spots on the two upper petals. Smells like an apple barrel.

PRETTY POLLY. Almond-scented, with crisp, fresh-looking heart-shaped leaves. Flowers rare, but they are a lovely pink when they do show.

P. scabrum, apricot-scented. The dark glossy, pointed leaves are deeply toothed. Large rose-coloured flowers.

Pungent-scented Pelargoniums

P. abrotanifolium. Finely cut leaves, with tiny white flowers faintly veined with red. A strong aromatic scent.

CAPRI. Large, crisp, crinkled leaves. Of mild scent. Crimson flowers.

CLORINDA. Eucalyptus scent. A compact plant with oak-shaped leaves and large pink flowers.

P. dennisianum, 'Round Leaf Balm'. Large, fragrant leaves. Of spreading growth, free flowering. The lavender, upper petals being brushed purple.

P. filicifolium. Erect branching habit. Well cut foliage; small orchid purple flowers.

P. grossularioides, 'Gooseberry Geranium'. Woody, bushy plants. The deep green leaves are blotched with yellow. Resembles the gooseberry bush.

FAIR ELLEN, a form of *quercifolium.* Purple marked, rough-textured leaf. Sticky stem and leaves. Lavender flowers, spotted purple.

P. ignescens, 'Mrs. Taylor'. Crinkly leaves on a spreading plant with bright red flowers.

OLD SCARLET UNIQUE. Hairy greyish leaves having pungent scent. Large flowers, scarlet with black markings.

P. quercifolium. Spreading plant with rough, dark green, oak-shaped leaves having a brown zone.

P. quercifolium, 'Skeleton's Unique'. Dark green leaves with brown zone. Deep orchid flowers marked purple. Of prostrate growth.

P. quercifolium giganteum, 'Giant Oak'. Coarse and tall growing having small rose flowers. Deep purple-veined leaves.

P. quercifolium pinnatifidum, 'Sharp-toothed Oak'. Purple-marked medium sized leaves. Pale pink flowers deeply marked rose.

P. quercifolium prostratum, 'Prostrate Oak'. A low growing plant with oak-shaped leaves having light brown zone. Deep orchid flowers.

P. rapaceum, 'Mrs. Kingsley'. The small ruffled and silvered leaves remind one of parsley. Red flowers.

STAGHORN OAK. Oak-shaped leaves with purple veining, lavender flowers.

P. viscosum, 'Pheasant's Foot'. The deeply cut leaf has the appearance of a pheasant's footprint. Light orchid flowers veined purple. Strong scent.

Pelargonium parviflorum has the common name of the 'Coconut-scented geranium'. This is one of the species which does not look at all like a pelargonium, in fact, as the first leaves appear they remind one of clover. The first true leaf, although small is of an attractive fan-like shape. Once the seedlings are well established, they grow rapidly, and when about 6 inches high, they begin to branch out into a number of individual stems.

As the plant becomes larger and matures, it throws out additional long, graceful stems which are sparsely dotted with a few leaves. At intervals, sprays of tiny white flowers feathered with maroon lines, are produced and growth is fairly rapid. The flowers although small, appear with great regularity. The seed pod ripens and eventually splits in the same way as most pelargoniums, each individual seed being carried away by its silken parachute and thereby spreading this fragrant plant over a wide area.

As in the case of almost all geraniums, the seeds are hardy and seem to come through quite low soil temperatures, which the plants certainly would not stand. Wherever a lovely spreading semi-trailing plant is required for the summer garden, or for the greenhouse, *Pelargonium parviflorum* most suitably fills the need.

The fragrance of the foliage is like that of freshly opened coconuts and the leaves do not need to be crushed, or even pinched, for the fragrance to become noticeable. A mere brushing of the leaves with the hands or clothing will be sufficient to distribute the scent. Grown in window-boxes, in hanging baskets, or in pots on the window-sill, this is an altogether pleasing plant. It can be propagated from some of the may shoots which form and these root quite rapidly.

In the Geranium Society's Year Book for 1954, Mr. D. J. Styles, the chief analyst of the firm of William Ransome and Sons of Hitchin, Hertfordshire, which specializes in galenical work, contributed a masterful article on *The Oil of Geranium.* In it he showed that this oil is a colourless to yellowish-green volatile liquid, with a pleasant rose-like odour, which is why it is employed widely in the perfumery, cosmetic and soap industries. This oil is obtained by steam distillation from various species of pelargonium.

The variety used most for this purpose is *Pelargonium graveolens* but *P. radula, P. capitatum* and *P. terebinthinaceum* have also been used as a source of geranium oil. *P. odoratissium* and *P. fragrans* are regarded as unsuitable to cultivate for the purpose of oil production. Mr. Styles showed that the essential oil is contained in small glands $\frac{1}{15}$th to $\frac{1}{18}$th millimetre long, distributed over the green parts of the plant, particularly in the leaves, although a very small amount of oil has been found also in the flowers.

The herb or all the aerial part of the plants, is gathered for distillation a short time before the opening of the flowers. When the lemon-like odour of the plants changes to a rose-like perfume the leaves at the same time commence to turn yellow. The yield of oil varies according to climatic conditions, type of soil, altitude and local methods of distillation. It has been found that light, chalky, gravelly soil is best, clay soil not suiting the plants.

Geranium Crispum   *Photo H. Smith*

There are also a number of scented-leaved hybrids which have come from *P. domesticum*, and some other species, including *fulgidum*. Of these, 'California Brilliant' is of good appearance and habit of growth. The roundish leaves have a heart-shaped base with regular and sharply toothed markings. The cherry-red flowers pale toward the centre. Among other hybrids which have the influence of *P. domesticum* are 'Clorinda', 'Rollinson's Unique' and 'Mrs. Kingsley'.

12 Dwarf Geraniums

AMONG THE various groups into which pelargoniums are divided, the dwarf and miniature zonal varieties have a particular appeal. These are available in single and double flowering forms and the mature plants rarely exceed a height of 8 inches. These miniatures appear to have come from normal sized plants and not through any of the shorter growing pelargonium species.

Although there is evidence that miniature geraniums were known before the end of the eighteenth century, it was not until just over a hundred years ago that named sorts appeared in any great number.

At the beginning of this century the then famous geranium specialist, Cannell, offered a number of miniatures including 'Salmon Black Vesuvius'. During the last twenty-five years many new varieties have been introduced, particularly in this country and in the United States.

One great advantage of the miniature zonals is that one can have such a wide range of colour in foliage and flowers. They are ideal for the small greenhouse and the sunny indoor window-sill and can be grown out of doors during the summer. Habit of growth and flower formation varies greatly but all have short flower stems which of course help to make them so low growing. Like all geraniums, they need sun and will not flower well unless they have enough of it. Since they are naturally bushy plants, they rarely need to have their growing points pinched out or to be pruned in any way.

It is not unusual for miniature varieties to be kept in $2\frac{1}{2}$-inch pots for several years. There is little root room or soil in such small pots and after a year or two, the leaves are liable to become smaller and the stems somewhat gnarled. This does not prevent the plants flowering. Given slightly bigger pots, the plants remain more virile, although an annual spring top dressing of rich soil is beneficial. Watering needs watching and should be done with care.

Really established miniature geraniums in 3- or 4-inch pots can be a very pleasing sight, since well grown, they make shapely specimens of 6 to 8 inches in diameter and height.

The colour of the foliage varies greatly. Some have very dark green, almost black leaves. In others, the foliage is olive-green, silver marked or tricolour.

The following are among the best of the varieties being grown at the present time.

BLACK VESUVIUS. Single, orange-scarlet. Very free flowering. Although known for well over seventy years, it has never been plentiful.

Dwarf Geraniums

CLAUDIUS. Dark green, almost black foliage with black zone. Large flowers of white suffused and veined camellia-rose.

CALIGULA. Deep green leaves, small double, bright scarlet flowers.

DANCER. Large flowers and clusters of single salmon. The dark green leaves are borne on short-pointed stems.

DWARF MIRIAM BASEY. Deep green leaves and large single flowers. The lower petals are reddish-vermilion, the upper ones being white flushed and marked red. Raised by F. G. Read.

ELF. Golden tricolour, the greyish-green leaves having a wide yellow border, zoned scarlet with darker markings. Small scarlet flowers.

FAIRYLAND. Silver tricolour, small dark greyish-green foliage bordered ivory and prettily zoned with irregular splashes of rose-red. Small, single scarlet flowers. A slow grower.

FLIRT. Dark green of bushy habit. The double, cream flowers are heavily flecked with reddish-salmon.

FRIESDORF. Very dark olive-green leaves zoned black, often having a frilled appearance. The narrow petalled flowers are a deep rose-crimson.

FROLIC. The bushy plants have dark green foliage and double salmon-apricot flowers.

GILL. Small zoned, dark green leaves with a grey sheen, the large flowers are a distinct cherry-red.

GOBLIN. Dark green leaves and good sized double scarlet flowers.

GOLDEN HARRY HIEOVER. A little large to be classed as a true dwarf. The glossy yellow-green leaves have a distinct bronze zone. The vermilion flowers are produced on rather lax stems.

GRANNIE HEWITT. This is an old variety which forms an attractive bushy plant; the small, light green leaves being faintly zoned. The small double flowers are bright scarlet.

KLEINE LIEBLING. Sometimes known as Little Darling and Hal. Probably of German origin. The bushy, compact plants have bright green foliage and single flowers of rhodomine-pink marked white.

LYRIC. A fairly fast growing, dark-leaved variety with double flowers of orchid-pink marked white at the centre.

MADAME FOURNIER. Known in France nearly seventy years ago this is an easy to manage variety. The small, single scarlet flowers show up well against the almost black foliage.

MADAME SALLERON. Sometimes listed as 'Madame Salleroi' and 'Dandy'. Of dwarf, bushy habit, the plants are often greater in diameter than height. The light green foliage has an irregular cream margin. No flowers.

MEPHISTOPHELES. Almost black leaves. Considered by many growers to be better than the older 'Red Black Vesuvius'. It has smallish vermilion flowers.

NUGGET. A golden tricolour, the olive-green foliage having a wide clear yellow border sometimes with a faint brownish zone on the young leaves. Small, single, pale salmon flowers. A slow grower.

PIXIE. Strong growing. Dark foliage. Light salmon single flowers.

RACHEL. Neat habit. Well-formed geranium-like flowers.

RED BLACK VESUVIUS. Small, very dark leaves with broad black zone. The large single signal-red flowers are freely produced.

SALMON BLACK VESUVIUS. This also has very dark leaves and large single salmon-rose flowers.

Dwarf Geraniums

SILVER KEWENSE. A sport from Kewense and introduced by the Caledonian Nurseries in 1956. This miniature has green, silvery edged leaves, sometimes striped silver. The freely produced narrow petalled flowers are currant-red.

SPRITE. The small dark greyish-green leaves have a wide ivory-white border and are sometimes flushed coral during the winter. This pretty, bushy plant produces single salmon-coral flowers.

SWEET SUE. The light green leaves are zoneless. The single mandarin-red flowers have a faint purple shading and a white eye.

TIBERIUS. Very dark foliage and large single flowers of orient-red.

TIMOTHY CLIFFORD. Very dark foliage with a black zone. The beautiful rose-coloured flowers are marked a deeper pink.

TRAJAN. Another dark-leaved variety also with a black zone. The single, signal-red flowers have a small white eye.

TWINKLE. A bushy spreading plant with dark leaves and double coral-rose flowers.

VARIEGATED KLEINE LIEBLING. Is a smaller, slower growing sport from 'Kleine Liebling' introduced by Holmes Miller of California in 1956. The slightly ruffled greyish-green leaves have a white border. The smallish, single pink flowers are freely produced, the upper petals having a white base.

Cultivation

When received from the nurseries place dwarf varieties in $2\frac{1}{2}$- or 3-inch pots. Any moss or algae on top of the root ball should be scraped off. Small amounts of soil should be crumbled away from the top and bottom of the ball to loosen some of the roots. The plants should be potted to the depth that they were originally, with the finished soil level half an inch below the rim of the pot. It is important to pot firmly, the new soil being tamped with a small stick. Be

Dwarf Geraniums

Dwarf Geraniums

Dwarf Geraniums

sure that no leaf stalks are buried. Water the plants thoroughly as soon as potted.

Place the plants where they get plenty of sun and good ventilation with the pots shaded from the sun. If established plants do not flower freely, it is a sure sign that they are not getting enough sun. Best temperatures are 65 degrees to 70 degrees F. during day and 55 degrees F. at night, but large fluctuations can be tolerated.

Dwarf Geraniums must never be allowed to become completely dry. They should be kept moderately moist at all times, but not soaking wet. They should be watered thoroughly when they are watered, with enough water poured on top of the soil so that a little will drain through the bottom of the pot. Do not let water stand in a saucer under the pot. The leaves should be kept dry except for an occasional washing in bright weather to remove dust. The small pots dry out quickly, and must be looked at often.

The Dwarf Geraniums will need feeding when grown as recommended, but should be fed only when the plant growth indicates the need. Abnormally slow, hard growth, small leaves, poor leaf colour, and loss of lower leaves are signs of need of feeding. Leaf colour is the most sensitive indicator. Feed by watering thoroughly with a weak solution of one of the soluble complete fertilizers. Plants that are watered every day may need feeding every two or three weeks. Less is needed in winter. It is easy to over-feed when the light is poor.

New Hybrids

Foremost among modern pelargonium breeders is F. G. Read of Brundall, the raiser of Miriam Basey and who specialises in dwarf zonal varieties and who has been very successful in exporting large quantities of seed to the U.S.A. and other countries.

Apart from the Little Read's seed strain his specialities include the Norwich Dwarfs a strain in which the foliage is golden yellow, some with bronze zones and others almost zoneless. New colours are regularly appearing in the seedlings and there is evidence that the coloured leaved range of fixed named varieties will be greatly widened.

Golden Gleam dwarf hybrids is the name of a series of dwarf zonals some having almost golden foliage, others with varying bronze tones. All are of vigorous growth producing large trusses. Named varieties include Katryn Portas, fuchsine-pink and Sorento, pink, both having fine well shaped golden foliage.

Many other new strains and varieties are on the way and will undoubtedly be released within the next few years. For the time being Billie Read is an attractive dwarf double with burgundy-red flowers, and Jimmy Read is a vigorous dwarf of similar colouring, both with large handsome foliage.

The Secretary of The British Pelargonium and Geranium Society has also raised some first class hybrids, among these being: Ethel James, a seedling from Francis James. Very large single pink flower that does not shatter easily, therefore good for showing, almost a bi-colour at times. Barbara Clark, a golden-bronze with a large single pink flower. A good bedder which likes plenty of sunny weather. Gold Sovereign, small double red flowers with bright golden-bronze leaves. Foliage very good and stands out well in bad weather. Propagates easily. Yours Truly, a strong grower with very wide deep zone,

116

deep pink single flower, small pips, medium head. Silent Oaf, deep red large single flower, vigorous. Endless Joy (Frutetorum hybrid) Scarlet, crinkly leaves.

Deacon Geraniums

The Decon floribunda geraniums are an entirely new strain first exhibited at Chelsea in 1970. Raised by the Rev. S. P. Stringer of Suffolk they are considered to be his greatest achievement to date and have been exported under license to many countries.

Derived from a cross between a miniature and an ivyleaf they have a compact, bushy habit with no tendency to sprawl, and can be expected to carry several heads of flowers at the same time. Ideal for all purposes including the show bench.

Although Deacons are as easy or easier than most other geraniums to cultivate, the full benefit of the new strain can only be obtained if growing techniques are adjusted to suit their requirements, and the following paragraphs may be of assistance.

They are not miniatures. It is possible to produce a Deacon 4 ft. high if it is grown in a pot large enough, and under the correct conditions. In the greenhouse the size of the plant can be largely controlled by the size of pot in which it is grown, so take it up 1 in. at a time until it reaches the size you require.

Deacons are gross feeders and if starved soon show signs of deficiencies in the foliage. Regular feeding with a balanced feed is essential to maintain steady regular growth. Com-Pel is a specially balanced liquid feed for the pelargonium family and contains everything the plant needs including trace elements in the correct proportions.

The original Deacon varieties were named: Coral Reef, Mandarin, Fire Ball, Bonanza, Romance and Lilac Mist. A new range is now available including: Arlon, Barbecue and Flamingo.

13 Unusual varieties

Bird's Egg Geraniums

In these geraniums there are small, rose-red spots on the petals, particularly the lower ones. This group originated towards the end of the last century. They were extensively grown at one time, but now are little known and consequently scarce.

BODE'S LIGHT PINK BIRD'S EGG. Single, pale pink, with all the petals, but particularly the lower ones, heavily spotted with small lavender-rose dots. Large clusters. A free flowering plant of moderately strong growth.

BODE'S CORAL BIRD'S EGG. Single, coral-rose with some white in the centre, all petals conspicuously spotted with rose-red. Large flowers and clusters. Free flowering, well-branched strong plants.

CURIOSA or DOUBLE PINK BIRD'S EGG. Orchid-pink with some white in the centre, all petals, but particularly the lower ones, spotted with small rose-red dots. Large flowers in very large clusters. A free flowering, large plant. The spots are not so conspicuous in this variety as in the others, but the flowers are really good.

MRS. J. J. KNIGHT. Single, very pale pink with all petals, but particularly the lower ones, heavily spotted with small rose dots. Very free flowering with good clusters. Slow growing, compact plants, but probably the best Bird's Egg geranium. Still rare.

SINGLE PINK BIRD'S EGG. Single, rose with some white in the centre. All petals, but particularly the lower ones, conspicuously spotted with small rose-red spots. Medium sized flowers. Free flowering compact plants.

SKYLARK. Single white Bird's Egg; compact habit, faintly tinged pink, spotted carmine.

Cactus-flowered Geraniums

These geraniums have narrow, rolled and twisted petals, of the type found in the cactus dahlias, and so are called cactus-flowered. They originated about 1900. There were once a considerable number of varieties, both single and double, but most of them are no longer grown in this country. Lately there has been a revival of interest, and a number of new varieties have been produced. The cactus-flowered geraniums are sometimes called Poinsettia geraniums, from the names of some of the older varieties.

DOUBLE POINSETTIA or ROSETTE. Deep red with narrow, rolled and twisted petals. Large flowered. A slender stemmed plant that needs pinching

Bird's Egg   Jeanne

Fig. 6.   Geraniums of unusual shape

Mr. Wren   Poinsettia

to keep it compact. Flowers very freely.

MISCHIEF. Double, orange-scarlet with narrow, rolled and twisted petals. Flowers well with medium sized clusters on short stalks. Leaves small, dark olive to blackish-green or maroon, depending on cultural conditions. Semi-dwarf habit, but not so small as the true dwarfs. An easily grown novelty that is decidedly different.

MORE MISCHIEF. Double, pale shrimp, pencil-veined deep salmon. Old flowers darker. Narrow, rolled and twisted petals. Bushy, semi-dwarf plant with blackish-green leaves. A sport of 'Mischief', and identical except for the flower colour. Interesting and attractive.

NOEL. Double white with narrow, rolled and twisted petals. Fairly large flowers of good substance. Strong bushy plants that flower well. This is the strongest growing of the cactus-flowered geraniums. The petals of 'Noel' are broader than those of 'Puff'.

PINK POINSETTIA. Double, light orchid-pink with a little white in the centre. Narrow, rolled and twisted petals. Compact plant with lots of flowers.

PUFF. Double white with narrow rolled and twisted petals. Good sized flowers in medium clusters. The petals are very narrow, and the flowers are not too full—desirable features in this class. Small, compact, bushy plants that flower freely. Ideal for a pot plant.

RED SPIDER, single intense scarlet with narrow, rolled petals. The free flowering plant has dark olive-green to blackish-green leaves. Of semi-dwarf habit, but considerably larger than the true dwarfs. An easily grown and unusual geranium.

SILVER STAR, single white with narrow, somewhat rolled petals. The petals are less rolled and wider than 'Puff'. Small, compact, but bushy, free flowering plants. 'Silver Star' is an attractive novelty.

SOUTHERN CROSS, double, salmon-coral with narrow, rolled and twisted petals. Unusually large flowers and clusters for this group. Medium to large plants, flowering freely.

STARLET, double rose-salmon with narrow rolled petals. Nice colour and good form. Medium sized plants.

STAR OF PERSIA, double purple-crimson, with narrow rolled petals. Large flowers of striking colour. Medium to strong growing plants.

119

Carnation-flowered Geraniums

In these geraniums, the margins of the petals are toothed, so that the flowers somewhat resemble small carnations, sweet williams, and pinks.

CERISE CARNATION. Double, cerise to light crimson, the edges of each petal being sharply toothed. Medium sized flowers in large clusters. Freely produced, the flowers are the most carnation-like of all in this group.

JEANNE, single, salmon, the edges of each petal sharply toothed. Small flowers in good clusters. Free flowering, bushy plants. An interesting variety, sometimes known as 'Sweet William'.

MADAME THIBAUT, single, white, changing to pink, the edges of each petal being sharply toothed. The flowers open pure white with a few rose-red veins at the base of the upper petals, and gradually change to pale pink, pink, or rose. Small flowers in good clusters. Odd and interesting. This variety too, has been called 'Sweet William'.

PRINCESS FIAT, raised in California in 1940. Double, soft shrimp-pink shading white at the toothed margins.

New Life Geraniums

This group originated with the introduction of the variety 'Vesuvius' in 1868. 'Vesuvius' soon produced a double-flowered sport, called 'Wonderful'. Some time prior to 1884, 'Vesuvius' produced another sport that had flaked or variegated flowers. This was called 'New Life', and is the most interesting of the group. 'New Life' soon sported again, and still does, fairly frequently.

About 1892, 'Wonderful', the double-flowered sport of 'Vesuvius', produced a sport with variegated flowers and was called 'Double New Life'. Although the flowers are quite different in each case, the plants are all the same, healthy and vigorous, but bushy and compact, and very free flowering. All do well both as pot plants and in the garden.

DOUBLE NEW LIFE. Double, scarlet and white flowers, some petals all scarlet, some all white or pinkish, others part scarlet and part white. Small flowers with many narrow petals. Very free flowering, compact plant. Frequently listed as 'Stars and Stripes'.

NEW LIFE. Single, scarlet flecked and striped with white. Occasional flower may be all scarlet, or all white with a pink centre, or part of a flower may be of one kind and part another. No two are alike. The flowers are of a nice round form, small to medium in size, and freely produced in good clusters that last a long time. The plant is compact and bushy, and easily grown. This very interesting old-time variety has become very scarce.

PHLOX NEW LIFE. Single, white, sometimes slightly flushed pink, with soft coral eye in the centre. Small to medium flowers of good form in fine clusters that last well. The plant is of the same compact, free flowering habit as the others. This is a sport of 'New Life', the extreme extension of the *phlox* pattern often seen in parts of the New Life flowers. It is of interest not only for its origin, but also as an attractive flowering geranium.

VESUVIUS. Single, scarlet, small to medium flowers in nice clusters, that last well. Plant of the same habit as the others. This variety occasionally appears as a 'reversion' from any of the others. 'Vesuvius' is of particular interest as the original variety from which this group developed, but it is also a useful scarlet-flowered variety when a compact, bushy plant is desired. It is *not* the same as the dwarf variety, 'Black Vesuvius'.

Unusual varieties

Phlox-Eye Geraniums

This is a small section of geraniums originating in the United States, many of the varieties being produced by the late Ernest Rober, at one time a well-known breeder and grower. These varieties are characterized by comparatively small single flowers, each of which has a round eye in the centre, the colour of this eye being different from that of the petals.

Among good varieties which are available in America, but not often in this country, are the following:

EDEE, orchid-pink with a prominent white eye.

PALE PHLOX, white flowers with a rose-pink centre.

PINK PHLOX, light pink with deep pink eye.

PHLOX EYE. The white flowers have a showy vermilion centre.

ROSE PHLOX, soft rose-pink, with darker centre.

Rosebud Geraniums

In this section the flowers never open wide, so that they resemble clusters of tiny, half-opened roses. They are all very double flowers, with the stamens and pistils replaced by many small petals. The name 'Rosebud' has been used in geranium literature for well over 100 years, although the old varieties have been lost.

APPLE-BLOSSOM ROSEBUD. Very double, white with distinct rose-red edging, green centre, and some green stripes. Mature flowers vary from rosebud form to almost fully open form. Medium sized flowers which last a long time. Strong plants, very unusual, flowers well.

PINK ROSEBUD. Very double, rose-red to cerise-red on the inside of the petals, considerably lighter, sometimes light pink, on the outside. Mature flowers hold the rosebud form. Strong plants.

RED ROSEBUD. Very double, red, possibly slightly scarlet. Mature flowers are more open than rosebuds, but still not fully expanded. Flowers are small, neat, and of fine substance. Medium size plants. Flowers freely, and is interesting and attractive. Also called 'Scarlet Rosebud'.

'Salmon Rosebud' and 'Vermilion Rosebud' are similar to the preceding varieties excepting for colour.

PURPLE RAMBLER. Royal purple. This makes bushy plants with many buds on each stem.

RED RAMBLER. Scarlet with pale pink markings on reverse of petals.

Unique Geraniums

The Unique Hybrids which are of shrubby, slender stemmed growth, have been in cultivation for well over a 100, perhaps 150 years, although there are only a few varieties that are at all well known today. They are useful for bedding purposes and authorities believe that to secure this group of plants, *Pelargonium fulgidum* was much used as a parent.

Varieties in this section, all of which have a charm of their own and of which the deeply lobed leaves usually emit a scent, include the following:

AURORE. Orient-red with darker markings.

CLARET ROCK. Tyrian-rose, feathered purple.

CRIMSON UNIQUE. Of medium size, crimson flowers marked black.

MADAME MONIN. Dark green leaves, the broad rose petals being shaded and veined red.

MRS. KINGSBURY or MRS. KINGSLEY. Rich green foliage, the tyrian-rose flowers being feathered purple.

PATON'S UNIQUE. An old variety of rather lax habit. The rose flowers are flushed red.

ROLLISON'S UNIQUE. One of the best known in this section. The lobed leaves are scented, hairy and toothed, the crimson flowers being marked purple.

SCARLET UNIQUE. This often makes bushy specimens 4 or 5 inches high. The foliage is well lobed with ruffled edges, the flowers being scarlet feathered with purple. This is much more like *P. fulgidum* than most of the other Unique varieties.

SELECT STORKSBILL. An old variety with pink flowers blotched and marked deep crimson.

SHRUBLAND PET. Of spreading habit, although somewhat sparse in flowering. The colour is rosy-red veined and feathered deep purple.

WHITE UNIQUE. Probably the largest in this group forming branching, woody, short-jointed stems. The three-lobed leaves are faintly scented, the flowers being white, very lightly tinted or marked purple.

Another most interesting, even if little known section of dwarf pelargoniums, are the Langley-Smith hybrids, named after the late Mr. Langley-Smith of Catford, who raised them.

Although sometimes listed as a new section with the date of introduction from the mid-1930's onwards, there seems to be evidence that this group of dwarf varieties is really a re-development of a range known nearly a century and a half ago as Angeline pelargoniums. These it seems, were believed to be forms of *P.* × *dumosum* and certainly the Langley-Smith hybrids show some evidence of the character of *P.* × *dumosum*.

It therefore seems appropriate that these plants are now identified by some specialist growers under the name of Angel pelargoniums. They usually grow 8 to 10 inches high, the blotched or feathered petals being well formed and overlapping, to make a well-shaped, pleasing flower. In this and other respects, these plants often look like miniature regal varieties.

They are first class for pot work in the greenhouse or for edgings for tubs and other large containers of the normal sized zonal varieties. Although small growing and compact, they are most free flowering and can be depended upon to give an abundance of colour.

The best known variety is 'Catford Belle', with purplish flowers. 'Mrs. Dumbrill' is mauve with purple markings and 'Rose Bengal' is rose-purple with paler edges.

Tuberous rooted Pelargoniums

Although the majority of pelargoniums are fibrous rooted, there are in fact, quite a number of species which are tuberous rooted. Many of these are interesting, some being scented in the evening and taking in quite a good range of colours.

P. apiifolium, has short thick stems with slender, hairy branches, the smooth leaves being much divided. The dark purple flowers have paler margins and are long spurred. The origin of this species is somewhat obscure, although it is known to have been in cultivation since early in the nineteenth century

P. × *ardens*. This is a deciduous hybrid, which has also been grown in this country since early in the nineteenth century. It is reckoned to be a hybrid between *P. fulgidum* and *P. lobatum*. It produces short, fleshy, knobbly stems with quite large, hairy leaves, usually divided into five lobes. The good sized, scarlet flowers which have dark red spots on the upper petals, are borne in small umbels.

P. bicolor. The origin of this is obscure, and it is possibly a hybrid, having been in cultivation for nearly 200 years. The upright stems grow to a height of 15 to 18 inches, the lobed leaves being coarsely toothed. The deep purple flowers have long stems.

P. bowkeri. The leaves, sometimes 10 to 12 inches long, are usually made up of very slender segments. The tall flower stems carry a dozen or more yellowish flowers which are tinged purple, and usually sharply fringed. Can sometimes be seen growing at Kew Gardens, although it is not really well known. It forms really large tubers.

P. fulgidum, makes short thick growths, the rather tender-looking three-lobed leaves being covered with heavy silvery hairs. The tall branching flower stems carry umbels of showy red flowers, usually veined brownish-red and having long spurs. This species is a native of South Africa, where it thrives in sun and sandy soil. It has been grown in Britain for more than 240 years. This species has had a considerable effect upon the development of a number of hybrids in the Domesticum group, and its influence is not difficult to recognize in such varieties as 'Mrs. Kingsbury', 'Shrubland Pet', etc.

P. gibbosum is probably the best known of the tuberous rooted varieties. It forms stems up to nearly 3 feet high, and has fleshy, woody swelling nodes. Because of these, it is often known as the 'gouty' geranium. The rather smooth fleshy leaves have up to seven lobes, which are well toothed. The greenish-yellow flowers, again with long spurs, are produced plentifully in umbels which arise from the leaf axils. This variety has been grown in England for more than 250 years and it loses its leaves in winter.

P. glaucifolium. This is somewhat like *gibbosum*, although the foliage is hairy. It is reckoned to be a hybrid of *P. gibbosum* and *P. lobatum*. Sometimes known as the black-flowered pelargonium, it produces many dark maroon flowers most of which have greenish-yellow margins to the petals.

P. pinnatum will often produce really large tubers, the growth being of rather stunted appearance. It forms a number of leaflets, the flower stems reaching a height of 10 to 12 inches, each pinkish-buff petal being spotted or marked with carmine. Long spurred.

P. rapaceum, this again does not produce stems of any great size, appearing as an under-developed plant. The rather heavy leaves are well divided. The 12-inch flower stems carry small pinkish-yellow flowers of which the upper petals are streaked with carmine and slightly reflexed. This species is very rare in cultivation.

P. × *rutaceum*. Another hybrid, the parents this time being *P. gibbosum* and *P. multiradiatum*. The stems of this plant are thickened, the hairy leaves being deeply divided and toothed. The dark maroon flowers are often edged with greenish-yellow, and they frequently emit a most pleasant fragrance at night.

P. triste. This is fairly well known, and produces tubers not unlike those of small potatoes. The large leaves are often as much as a foot long, and are well divided, the stems being short and fleshy. The tall flower stems produce many brownish flowers with yellow margins, the long stem adding to the attractiveness of this species, which is sometimes known as the 'sad' geranium.

14 Pelargonium species

PELARGONIUM SPECIES are those members of the pelargonium genus which are found in the wild and which come true when raised from seed. There are, in fact, a large number of species, the exact figure being unknown, although it is certainly over 200. For convenience, botanists have grouped the species together according to their shared characteristics. Each of these groups has been given an appropriate Latin name, so that each section may be divided.

It is generally reckoned that the pelargonium genus is divided into fifteen sections, although this number is by no means final and it may well be that there will be other divisions recognized by botanists before long. Some of these sections do, of course, contain unusual species which are rarely seen outside Botanical Gardens.

The genus pelargonium has its centre of distribution in South Africa, and it extends to the east coast of Africa as well as into Arabia and Western India. There are a limited number of species to be found in Australia and Madagascar, while one occurs on Tristan da Cunha.

There is tremendous diversity in the species, some producing almost bulbous-like roots, others are of straggly growth, and those which will scramble over bushes. The modern varieties now so well known to us have been created from the union of a number of species, and undoubtedly *P. cucullatum* and *P. betulinum* have had a large part to play in the production of the regal or show varieties. In the case of the zonal sorts, which includes the popular bedding varieties, *P. inquinans* and *P. zonale,* and many others, have been used in hybridizing to form such splendid plants as we see in our gradens today.

Since we are not dealing with the subject in a technical or botanical sense, we are here concerned only with a few of the better known species, many of which are still quite rare in this country.

Pelargonium angulosum forms a shrubby, erect, much-branched plant, the leaves being very hairy and usually quite rough to the touch. It is a native of the mountainsides of the Cape and nearby districts of South Africa, where it grows 3 to 4 feet high. It produces panicles of four to six purplish-pink flowers which have darker streaks.

P. betulinum forms a very attractive plant with a low growing shrubby habit. The erect slender stems carry smallish hairless leaves. The lavender-pink, medium sized flowers having upper petals which show dark veins. It can be found growing wild in the sandy coastal strips on the Cape peninsula and is known to be one of the parents of *P.* × *domesticum.*

P. cucullatum. This also is to be found growing very freely on the hills and mountainsides of the Cape peninsula. It makes tall-growing shrubby, branched plants at least 4 to 5 feet high. The freely produced flowers have large, crimson double petals the upper ones being feathered purple. This too, is one of the parents of *P. × domesticum.*

P. inquinans, is to be found chiefly in the eastern parts of the Cape Province where it grows in fairly shallow ground. The smooth woody branched plants have soft, rather hairy, shallowly lobed leaves. Plants grow up to 3 feet high and carry good sized umbels of vermilion-red flowers, although there seems some evidence that pink blooms are sometimes produced. This is probably the most important ancestor of *P. × hortorum.* There are records of its being in cultivation for well over 240 years, and it is undoubtedly one of the earliest of all pelargoniums referred to in literature.

P. carnosum is a native of dry districts of Cape Province. It forms thickish, succulent stems, the branches being swollen at the joints. It produces panicles of six to eight white, or mauvish-white flowers.

P. cotyledonis, popularly known as 'old man live for ever', produces dwarf

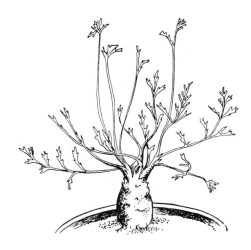

Fig. 7. *Pelargonium ferulaceum*

spreading, short, succulent woody stems. The bright leaves are slightly hairy underneath, the small white flowers being produced on 12-inch stems.

P. ferulaceum. This grows naturally in coastal areas of South Africa where there is low rainfall. Like *P. carnosum,* it has swollen stout stems of branching habit, the long fleshy leaves being well divided. It has small whitish flowers on 12- to 18-inch stems. In its natural habitat it seems to be particularly happy where it has the shelter of shrubs. During the dry season when the plants are leafless they look very much as if they are dead. The shade of shrubs seems to elongate the stems, so that in time, the plants become almost as broad as they are tall.

P. gibbosum has the popular name of the Knotty or Gouty Storksbill; it has been grown in England for more than 250 years. The long flower stems carry ten or more small yellowish flowers which have a most attractive perfume reminding one of honeysuckle. It is only during the hours of darkness that this scent is noticeable. Then, it still persists even when the flowers are under artificial light. The stem is long and thin, with quite large swollen nodes, the habit of the plant is more or less upright, although it can be used as a trailing plant in the greenhouse, The leaves too, are quite attractive, the fresh green colour assuming a steel-grey shade.

This species will root readily if cuttings are made in the autumn, and when they are severed through the node and placed in sandy compost. *P. gibbosum* has tuberous roots and when raised from seeds these roots develop quickly, although they are slower from the cuttings.

P. echinatum forms tuberous roots and shrubby, rather succulent erect growth. The slightly lobed, dark green leaves are soft to the touch. It produces branched heads of white, pink and purple flowers, which are often marked crimson or purple. A form, or clone, known as *P.* × *'Miss Stapleton'*, has great appeal. This produces intense magenta flowers on rigid sprays, shaded in age to mauve. The white form *P. e. album* is a perfect companion to this variety.

P. denticulatum forms shrubby, erect, slightly branched plants. The dark green, large, cut leaves, being balsam-scented. It produces pale lilac flowers, having a purple blotch, although it is the scented foliage for which this plant in its many forms is cultivated.

P. capitatum, known in cultivation since 1690, forms shrubby, rather spreading plants, with finely lobed leaves, which are delightfully rose-scented. The small-rosy-purple flowers have dark veins. When seen growing in its natural habitat this plant is said to resemble a small green hedgehog, because of the dense head of seed pods which form after the flowers are over.

P. crispum also forms shrubby erect branched plants, the small leaves being cut and curved, while they emit a rather pleasant lemon scent. The flowers are pale violet, lined purple. This is a species of which there appears to be many forms, which has led to some confusion in identification.

P. frutetorum. This forms scrambling, slender fleshy growth. The five-lobed leaves having dentate edges and being strongly zoned in fact, this is a species which is more zoned even than zonale itself.

P. graveolens. A shrubby erect, branching species having hairy leaves of grey-green colour, which are rose scented. The small pink flowers are veined and spotted purple. This undoubtedly is the ancestor of many of the scented-leaved varieties and of the oil producing kinds.

P. hirsutum produces long stalked leaves which vary in shape all being pubescent. The branching stems bear flowers of rosy-white veined pink or rose, although in some cases, the colour is purplish-black. It may well be that there is more than one species generally recognized and distributed as hirsutum.

P. hybridum. Often known and regarded as *P. salmoneum*, this plant has slender, erect stems with rather glaucous fleshy, pubescent leaves. The long salmon-pink petals have darker veins. Although not easy to obtain, seed is sometimes available and the plants raised come true.

P. peltatum has slender smooth stems, the young growth being succulent. The stems branch well, the thick fleshy leaves being bright green. This is the species which is considered to have contributed much to the present-day Ivy-leaved varieties. The mauve-white petals are tinted and spotted carmine.

P. rapaceum, a less common species, with long hairy, flower stems and umbels of rosy-white or flesh-coloured flowers with dark mottlings. There is also another form having primrose-yellow spotted flowers. Its natural habitat is on the dry, stony mountainsides near Cape Town where it grows 9 to 12 inches high.

P. monstrum. This forms shrubby swollen, rather succulent growth, with thickish branches well furnished with dark green, zoned leaves. The pale pink flowers have darker veins on their upper petals.

P. acetosum is another shrubby species, with rather slender erect stems. The rather long and narrow petals are porcelain-rose with deeper veinings. Although known since 1795, this is quite a rare species in cultivation.

P. tetragonum forms succulent, erect, branching plants, the stems often being 'square'. The lobed, dark green leaves, are rather fleshy and hairy and have a dark central blotch. Each stem carries two or three flowers which are rosy purple, with darker featherings, the lower petals being a paler colour.

Fig. 8.   Pelargonium stenopelatum

P. triste is said to have been introduced into England in 1632 by John Tradescent. This has a tuberous branching root system. It is almost stemless, the short decumbent growths forming large pinnate leaves. The stems produce many flowers of which the small petals are a brownish-purple, with yellow

127

margins. These flowers are very sweet scented after sunset. A form known as *flavum*, sometimes listed as a separate species, has greenish-yellow flowers with finely cut leaves.

P. zonale is probably the best known species and certainly the most widespread in South Africa, from whence it has been distributed into many parts of the world. It forms semi-shrubby growth, the branching plants bearing cordate leaves, somewhat hairy and zoned, although strangely enough, not so deeply zoned as some other species. Typical plants bear purplish flowers with lighter edges, although the colour does vary to shades of red.

P. paradoxum is a succulent, sturdy, branching species, growing about 1 foot high. The glaucous-green, much divided leaves are very brittle and when growing in its natural habitat in Namaqualand, thrives in the full sun. When the leaves fall, the stems are hard to distinguish from the background of the grey sands. If grown in more moist conditions the foliage becomes most luxuriant. Although known in this country for over fifty years, it is very little grown. The white flowers are produced in umbels of four to ten florets.

P. crithmifolium. This is another species with succulent rather straggling stems and fleshy leaves. Growing up to 2 feet high, it produces small umbels of flowers on which the white petals are spotted red at the base.

P. alternans. This is another succulent branching species, of short rather rough, knotted growth. The small rather narrow white petals are somewhat reflexed, having red lines toward the centre. Growing only 6 inches high, this species has been known about 170 years and whereas in its native habitat in stony or rocky slopes, the flowers are produced when the leaves have completed growth, when this species is cultivated, the flowers usually appear at the same time as the leaves.

P. moniliforme. This is a dwarf, tuberous rooted species occuring frequently in Namaqualand, where it seems to like stony or gravel ground. The leaves form rosette-like growth and the creamy-white flowers have a red blotch on each petal. Since this is such a dwarf growing plant, often only 2 or 3 inches high, it can easily be overlooked, especially when out of flower. It seems to like a long rest period so that it dries off well. It has been found that when grown in pots, the lower leaves are inclined to become too dried out, whereas of course, grown on the hillsides, the ground remains cool below the surface.

P. lobatum forms large, uneven tubers. It is almost stemless, the leaves usually being tri-lobed and rather soft and felty underneath. The flower stems grow 15 to 18 inches high, the very dark coloured petals having a yellowish base and margin. This species usually emits a scent as darkness falls. It is found growing naturally on the dry, clayey somewhat rocky ground in the Cape Town area.

P. spinosum. This is of shrubby growth, the much branched plants carrying rigid leaf stalks, bearing greyish-green rather brittle foliage. The leaves have a pungent smell when bruised. The flowers, which form in large clusters are white, sometimes with faintly purple lines on the petals. The plant varies in height frequently being only 1 foot and on other occasions it can be seen much higher. It seems to thrive in the hottest of sun, not flagging in any way. This is another species found growing wild in Namaqualand.

P. mirabile is also known as *P. hemisphericum*. This species forms large, branched, half-spherical bushes 12 inches or more in height and width. The succulent greyish-brown stems are much branched. Since it is leafless for much of the year, it is not particularly interesting, but in Namaqualand, after the rains have fallen, it soon becomes clothed in attractive leaves followed by many white and pink flowers. It is unlikely to be seen in this country apart from specialist collections.

A plant which is rarely, if ever, seen outside botanical gardens is *Pelargonium endlicherianum*, which I believe to be the only hardy species in existence. It is a native of the limestone Alps of the Cilician Taurus and will actually live a long time in quite exposed positions.

Perhaps the name itself is one of the reasons why the plant is not better known, or more frequently grown. If it were seen more often, it would be much more widely cultivated by gardeners, since it is not only hardy, but beautiful. Undoubtedly, although it is now so rare, means would be found, if the demand was sufficient, to enable nurserymen to grow and offer this species. The plants like well-drained, fairly rich soil in which there is a good lime content and the more sun they have the better.

The plants develop into leafy bushes of which the rather soft, but typically geranium-like leaves are well scalloped and strongly aromatic. The continuously produced flower stems, usually from 12 to 18 inches high but sometimes more, carry clusters of from three to six clear rosy pink flowers which look well both when grown in the border or in the rock garden. The formation of the blooms always commands a second look on account of the upper petals being so much larger than the lower ones. Coconut fibre or something similar placed around the plants in late autumn, will give protection from the most severe winter weather.

The foliage of this plant, which received an Award of Merit as long ago as 1901, usually develops attractive autumn colourings and this is another reason why it deserves greater attention.

15 Flowering and care in Winter

IT IS one thing to say that geraniums will flower in the winter but quite another thing to get them to do so, for although it is not at all difficult to have colour from March until October, for the remaining months, more care is necessary. Provided certain simple precautions are put into operation and the right varieties are depended upon, some geraniums can be relied upon to produce blooms throughout the shortest days.

Very often, healthy plants which have given of their best during the dark days, will continue to flower well the following summer without showing any signs of loss of vitality. Some of the smaller, young plants, which have been bedded out during the summer can be potted up for greenhouse work and will normally flower again after the check of transplanting has been overcome.

It is best to take cuttings specially for the purpose of getting winter flowering plants. Any grower who has the means of providing sufficient heat to exclude frost and keep out damp can do this. In fact, a lot of heat is not required, since the plants prefer a buoyant atmosphere, although of course, frosts will destroy the plants.

Occasionally, a successful show of winter blooms can be had from early autumn-struck cuttings, but best results undoubtedly come from young plants secured in March and April. It is important to take out the growing tips once the cuttings have rooted, to induce the formation of laterals which makes for good bushy, free flowering plants.

Experiments have been made with artificial lighting and these have certainly proved that some varieties, at least, respond well to such treatment, the foliage usually being a better colour and healthier looking than one normally gets in the winter. This system demands the removal of flower buds during the summer. Grown in this way, the blooms are often smaller and the colour paler than when grown naturally.

When many of the now popular winter flowering subjects were unknown, zonal pelargoniums occupied an important place in the greenhouse, conservatory or even windows, of those who required colour during the darkest days of the year, but the introduction of many other types of winter flowering plants has led to the neglect of zonal pelargoniums for this purpose.

It is only worthwhile trying to get the zonals to bloom in the winter. The other sections seem reluctant to do so and even with the zonals, care is necessary in selecting varieties. It has been noticed that single varieties will bloom before the doubles, and the crimson-purple sorts before the scarlets. The following, fully described in the chapter on varieties, have all proved to be reliable for flowering during the shortest days of the year: 'F. V. Raspail', which is smallish growing and of wiry appearance, 'Caroline Schmidt', 'Decorator', 'Double Henry Jacob', 'Notting Hill Beauty', 'Gustav Emich', 'Victory', 'King of Denmark', 'Lady Warwick', 'Paul Crampel' and 'Queen of the Whites'.

Regular ventilation, plenty of light and the removal of dead leaves are essential. Although water should be given as necessary to keep the plants in good condition, it must be kept down to the minimum. With the fairly low winter temperatures, there is always a greater possibility of mildew or decay setting in, should excessive moisture be given. If possible, give water from a tank inside the greenhouse; otherwise, use tap or rain water with the chill off.

It is a mistake to over-pot, for although one obviously wants to obtain plants as large as possible for winter flowering, much root room will encourage leaf and stem growth at the expense of flowers. Geraniums flower most freely in the winter when they are more or less potbound and the stems have slightly hardened. A really good show can be secured from plants in 4- or 5-inch-diameter pots.

Sometimes where larger plants are available to begin with, they can be put into bigger receptacles especially if they have a good-sized root system. Young plants should be in their flowering size pots not later than early October. The John Innes Potting Compost No. 2 will be found a most suitable rooting medium, or a simple mixture of three parts fibrous loam, one part peat and half part silver sand with a dusting of hoof and horn or bone meal will be found ideal. Additionally, a little mortar rubble or brick dust will be of great benefit.

It is also worthwhile giving each plant, in the late autumn, a pinch of fish manure or some other good organic fertilizer. This is far better than attempting to feed with forcing, quick acting fertilizers, which may bring the plants into bloom quickly, but which will quickly weaken and exhaust them.

The Rosebud group of varieties cannot be recommended for growing to flower in the winter. They sometimes produce buds, then fail to open properly, thus being most unattractive.

I am greatly indebted to Mr. A. C. Ayton, the Pelargonium Specialist of Southborough, Kent, for details of his method of ensuring the late winter flowering of pelargoniums. This is as follows:

The plants as sent out will be from cuttings taken in early June and will be from 3½-inch pots. As soon as the plants are received, put them into 5-inch pots, shade for one week to recover from the journey. Then place the plants in a greenhouse or heated frame, in a temperature of 45 to 50 degrees F.; keep well watered. Spray the plants with water overhead completely, twice a week until the buds appear. Increase the temperature to 50 to 55 degrees F. in November with as much light as possible. Artificial daylight can be applied for two or three hours a day with most beneficial results, at this stage.

The plants should be potted into John Innes Compost No . 2 and, one month after, be given a weak solution of a fertilizer such as Clays, every ten days.

As soon as the first flowers are over, pinch out the spent flower head to induce further blooms; they should then flower freely for a five- to six-week period.

If you do not require to pot these plants on to a larger size pot to make specimen plants next year, plant them out of doors in the garden in full sun at the end of May and then a further stock of cuttings may be taken at the end of June for the following winter's flowering.

The foregoing instructions are for Regal pelargoniums (*Pelargonium domesticum*) and may be reasonably applied to ordinary geraniums (*Pelargonium zonale*) with the exception that with varieties of the zonal types, all flowering buds should be removed which form before mid-October. Thereafter, all buds should be allowed to develop naturally. Full light and the given temperatures are necessary for success.

It is wise to remember that if you take the plants into the house for decoration they should be moved in just as the buds are opening and placed in full light, i.e. on the window-sill. Stand the plants in a cool, light airy shed for twenty-four hours before taking them indoors. You will find that this conditioning much improves the lasting qualities of these excellent plants.

The double and semi-double varieties of geraniums respond best to winter flowering treatment.

Since geraniums are one of the most widely grown pot plants it is usually the endeavour of the grower to bring them through the winter. During this period they certainly need careful maintenance to ensure their survival. They should be kept in the light as far as possible and this means that even in the greenhouse, the glass should be kept clean by washing it inside and out.

Young plants in particular, should be kept on the staging, preferably on a layer of coarse shingle where they will get the maximum benefit from winter light. The shingle ensures that surplus water drains away from the pots.

Although little moisture is necessary, when it is needed it should be given during the early part of the day. Throughout cold spells when the soil may even become frozen, watering should be discontinued and the atmosphere kept dry. If plants do become touched by frost, they should be kept out of the sun so that thawing becomes a gradual process.

Very often plants can be protected sufficiently by simply placing sheets of newspaper over the plants on any night when frosts are expected and this, with the absence of moisture, will usually bring them through cold spells.

Some ventilation is necessary, but it should not be given during very cold and foggy weather. If, of course, a night temperature of around 40 to 45 degrees F. (6-7 C.) can be maintained, the plants will be unharmed.

Decayed leaves and bracts should be removed and if there is the slightest sign of fungus or mildew of any kind, a dusting of yellow sulphur should be applied.

Where a number of cuttings remain in large receptacles they can be potted up singly in John Innes Compost No. 2 as soon as the days begin to lengthen. If the compost is nicely moist there should be no need to give a further application of water until rooting commences. This is seen by the plants becoming perky.

It is, I am sure, far better to plant as suggested, rather than to tie the roots in bundles and hang them in a shed or similar place. By keeping them in soil the stems remain perfectly plump whereas if they are out of the soil they are liable to shrivel.

It is certainly true that it is an old practice to take up the plants in the autumn, and hang them in sheds to dry, but it is definitely not, a wise or a successful method. The damp days of October and November encourage the development of fungus disease on the dying leaves and this quickly spreads to stem and roots and the plant is entirely consumed by decay.

16 The true hardy Geranium

THE LITTLE Herb Robert, *Geranium robertianum*, flourishes beneath hedge bases or in other shady roadside places. In addition, this and other attractive little species can frequently be found in hilly limestone districts, where they climb walls with ease and make a brave show for several months of the spring and summer. These cheerful little Cranesbills include the biennial *Geranium lucidum*, with small, bright rose coloured flowers which appear with great freedom along the 6- to 10-inch sprawling plant stems.

Another small flowered species, which makes neat little hummocks of growth, is *Geranium celticum*; it has long been known under that name, although some botanists now say that it is an albino form of *G. robertianum*. Amid the fern-like foliage, there are produced throughout the summer, numerous dainty, starry, white flowers on 3- to 4-inch stems. Since the plant thrives in a shady, moist position, the little white blossoms show up well.

Geranium dissectum, the cut-leaved Cranesbill, is of erect growth with red flowers. It is a common weed in some cornfields and likes limey soil. A profuse seeder, it carries many thousands of seeds which germinate freely.

The Dove's Foot Cranesbill, *Geranium molle*, is a small, much branched spreading plant, with stems rarely more than 6 inches long and it prefers poor, dry soil. The mauve flowers are freely produced. These Cranesbills should not really be allowed to establish themselves in the border, otherwise they become quite invasive.

Intriguing as these dainty wildings are, it is the larger growing, hardy Cranesbills, which are of the most value in the rock garden or front of the border, as well as in the wild garden.

The best of these I will now mention alphabetically and therefore not necessarily in order of merit. Although all are normally obtainable without difficulty, none are troublesome to grow. The majority will thrive in any good soil and full sun, while most will grow in semi-shade as well.

Geranium anemonifolium, which prefers a sunny, sheltered position, is perhaps the one which should be given a little more care in cultivation. Introduced from Madeira toward the end of the eighteenth century, it will thrive where there is very little soil, especially if given the protection of a wall. It forms large rosettes of showy leaves which colour up well, while from the tall branching stems, there appear very many crimson flowers.

G. argenteum has been grown here for more than 250 years, and is an indispensable rock plant. It has attractively cut leaves which are evergreen and these, as the name suggests, are of a silvery colouring. The 6-inch branching stems produce, just above the foliage, rich pink, saucer-shaped flowers and there are forms known as Lissadell variety, *purpureum* and *alanah*, which may all be synonymous, showing blooms which are a near-crimson colour. The white form, *album*, is less attractive, since it does not show up its blooms in such contrast to the foliage as do the pinks and crimsons.

G. armenum is strikingly handsome. Originating in Armenia, it will grow as much as 3 feet high when given a rich site. The freely produced, large flowers are of a real magenta shade which is unusual in flowers, the dark centre making the petal colour even more attractive. Not easy to interplant with other more brightly coloured such as the pinks and reds, *G. armenum* is most effective when given a niche of its own, where it can flower freely without becoming an eyesore against other plants. It is not invasive and does not require staking.

G. atlanticum from Spain and Morocco, although little known, is quite pretty, its purple-blue coloured flowers appearing on 12- to 18-inch stems, surrounded by well cut, anemone-like leaves. One of the earliest to bloom, it has curious tuberous roots. It does well on a hot, dry bank.

Altogether smaller growing, *G. cinereum* from the Pyrenees, is somewhat similar to *G. armenum* except in size. Easy to grow, it has greyish-green, cut leaves and cupped, rosy purple flowers on 6-inch stems. *G. cinereum album,* is a scarce form but most handsome and distinguished. It can only be increased by division and is therefore never likely to become common. It was this albino form of which Farrer said, 'It has purity, brilliance and charm beyond all others'.

G. dalmaticum is comparatively new to this country, and its name will suggest its origin. Its worth was recognized almost as soon as it reached British gardens, since it received an R.H.S. Award of Merit in 1940. Dwarf growing, it is ideal for the rock garden, forming low, shapely mats of well cut, glossy leaves, which take on pleasing autumn tints. The well-proportioned clear pink flowers are carried on stems of 6 to 8 inches, the prominent dark stamens and stigma, adding to the beauty of the blooms. Easy to grow in fairly light soil, in the open or on a wall, it is also admirable for growing in a pot or pan, while it is most suitable for the alpine house.

G. delavayi, although introduced by Père Delavay as long ago as 1886 and reintroduced from China by George Forrest, is still very rare. It throws up several loosely branched leafy stems 18 to 24 inches long, and flowers of a deep blackish-crimson, with a bright ruby stigma surrounded by golden anthers.

G. endressii from the Pyrenees is fine for making a bold display near the front of large borders or as a ground cover under and around shrubs. It grows in almost any soil, flowering freely both in full sun and partial shade. Its almost evergreen leaves often turn to pale gold and reddish shades in the autumn, while the abundantly produced raspberry-red flowers show from late May until prolonged frosts put an end to them for the season. A fine plant for the stream-side, it looks especially well when seen growing among ferns or Solomon's Seal. The variety 'A. T. Johnson' is similar but the flowers are a delightful shade of silvery pink. 'Rose Clair' is another form, in this case the flowers being rose-salmon with slight traces of veinings, which probably indicates the influence of *G. striatum* in its parentage. Various other hybrids often appear having more pronounced pencillings on the petals.

134   Best suited for growing in the wild garden is *G. eriostemon* from Russia. This

has purple coloured flowers on 12- to 18-inch stems. It is sometimes known as *G. platyanthum.*

A first-class species introduced by Reginald Farrer about 1817 has become widely known as *G. napuligerum,* although it is also frequently catalogued and referred to as *G. farreri,* which is now recognized as its rightful name (it is certainly easier to pronounce and remember!). A lovely dwarf apline, it thrives in well-drained soil in a sunny position, where early in the spring, it puts out clusters of ash-grey, deeply cut leaves. These are quickly followed by branching stems 3 to 4 inches high, which bear several large cup-shaped, apple-blossom-pink flowers, set off by prominent dark anthers. Given a gritty soil, in a sunny position, *G. farreri* rarely, if ever, fails to do well. An indispensable rock garden plant, it may be increased by division or more slowly from seeds.

G. grandiflorum, from northern Asia, grows to a height of about 12 inches, its woody stems creeping along the ground for some inches before it assumes an upright habit. The round and deeply cut foliage takes on handsome autumn tints. The large flowers, often 2 inches in diameter, are intense blue, lightly veined with crimson pencillings and deepening to red in the centre. This is a first class plant for the front of the border, for edging or massing among shrubs. It is easily increased by division in either the autumn or the spring and does well on most soils.

Flowering from early summer to late autumn is *G. grandiflorum alpinum,* sometimes known as Gravetye variety. Although several inches shorter than the type, it is of a rather spreading habit, and should therefore be given ample space to develop. It is however, so lovely that it is worth any trouble needed in restricting its growth. It likes sun and almost any type of soil, and shows its large clear blue flowers from early June until late September.

Ideal for the wild garden, *G. ibericum* continuously produces its rich violet-purple flowers on stems 18 to 24 inches high. *G. kotschyi* from Armenia, throws up many anemone-like leaves, which however, contrary to the majority of species, die down in the autumn. This species, too, has thick almost tuber-like roots, and throughout the early summer pushes up its 9-inch branching stems, of really large lavender-purple flowers, of which the petals are veined with deeper markings.

G. lancastriense, see *G. sanguineum var. lancastriense.*

G. lowei. Coming from the Canary Islands, this fine little plant grows to a height of 18 inches or more, and is often as large in diameter. The boldly cut, fleshy foliage assumes autumnal tints. In addition, it has good sized pinkish-red flowers with a musky scent and seeds itself freely.

G. macrorrhizum from the Balkans, forms low hummocks of rounded, light green scented leaves, which usually colour to shades of red in the late autumn. It is said that in some parts of the world it is grown for the extraction of its oils, whilst the fleshy rhizomes are used in the tanning of leathers. Growing about 1 foot high with fine pink flowers, it succeeds in all types of soil, excepting very dry positions. It is a most hardy perennial and useful as a ground carpeter.

It has several forms, including *var. album,* which with its inch-wide, snow-white flowers is always effective. *G. m. var. grandiflorum* is another fine form with clear pink flowers. 'Ingwersen's variety' has been known for well over forty years. This produces large flowers of the clearest rose-pink, while the foliage is most attractive. *G. maculatum* is regarded as a wild plant in North

135

America and has several popular names including 'Chocolate Flower' and 'Sailors Knot'. From the thickish root stock, there are produced handsome cut leaves and reddish-pink flowers 1½ inches in diameter.

G. malvaeflorum. This is usually listed as *G. atlanticum* (q.v.).

G. molle (*dissectum*) this is a native plant often known as the Dove's Foot Granesbill and Pigeon Foot. It produces quite tiny pink flowers which soon pass over and it is a plant which is only suitable for the wild garden.

G. napuligerum. The true species does not appear to be in cultivation and the plant often distributed under this name is *G. farreri.*

G. palustre is of rather sprawling habit, rarely more than 10 to 12 inches high. It produces a succession of large, rich carmine flowers which go on appearing until the autumn. The colour makes it a difficult plant to grow near many other brightly hued subjects.

G. phaeum is the 'Mourning Widow' geranium of Victorian times. It was so named because of its dark brown flowers, of which each petal has a white spot at the base. This species and its rare white form, *album*, grow approximately 15 to 18 inches high, and are of most easy culture.

The form known as *lividum* produces a long succession of really large flowers of grey-blue. They look especially good when seen growing among shrubs or in the wild garden, where the quiet colour gives a good tone to the surroundings.

The blue meadow cranesbill, *Geranium pratense*, although a wilding, is nevertheless a beautiful flower. Rather rampant in growth, unless kept under control, it looks well when planted in the front of the herbaceous border, where large, bowl-shaped flowers of clear blue with a white eye, show up to great advantage. There are now several cultivated forms which include 'Mrs. Kendall Clark', pale opal; 'Silver Queen', silvery-blue, on vigorous stems 30 inches or more high; and *album*, with large milk-white flowers on 2-foot stems.

In spite of its name, *Geranium pylzowianum* from China, is pretty. It has 1-inch wide, clear pink flowers on stems of about 4 or 5 inches. It is a deciduous species which forms a network of thread-like roots, which although they tend to roam, are so frail as not to cause trouble.

G. renardii from the Caucasus Mountains, forms tufts of deeply lobed, grey-green thick leaves. Produced on 6- to 9-inch stems, the charming lavender flowers appear throughout the summer and autumn.

Long known as the Bloody Cranesbill, *G. sanguineum* is of rather creeping habit, with crimson-magenta flowers. It is, however, the form known as *lancastriense* without which no rock garden is complete. Originally found on the Isle of Walney in Lancashire, the plants bear a very long succession of salmon-pink, cup-shaped flowers, set among the dark green leaves. Grown among grey foliaged plants, it is strikingly effective.

G. sessiliflorum nigricans, is a flat-growing species, of very easy culture. It has very dark foliage, made more prominent during the summer when the small white flowers develop. *G. striatum* of decumbent habit, produces from May to October, pretty pink flowers with dark veins.

G. sylvaticum is another native found mostly in the North of England, with purple-blue flowers, having crimson veins, and appearing on 2-foot stems during June and July. It is, however, the newer forms of this species, which are most worthwhile. These are *album*, 18 inches, the pure white flowers often having buds which are prettily tinted pale pink; *roseum*, an unusual clear rose-pink and *var. caeruleum* rich blue, white eye.

G. stapfianum, is a handsome little plant, with glossy green leaves which colour up in the autumn, and rosy-pink flowers on 4-inch stems. The form *roseum*, is similar, but the blooms are of a crimson-purple colour.

Another larger growing geranium is *viscosissimum*. It looks well towards the front of the herbaceous border, where it can have partial shade, and where it produces its 2-inch wide purple-red flowers on strong stems up to 2 feet in height.

G. tuberosum. This is a species widely spread around the drier Mediterranean regions. It is of little value as a garden plant since its flowers are so fleeting. It forms an underground root stock from which there arises stems of 8 or 9 inches bearing few leaves and flowers of an indifferent whitish colour stained with pink.

G. wallichianum was introduced to Britain from Nepal about 1819. Although when compared with some of the other species it is not outstanding, it is of value in that it is autumn flowering. It also starts into growth late in the spring at a time when one might be imagining that it has died. The flower stems are inclined to flop or sprawl about, while, the blooms themselves although large, are of an unattractive lilac-purple shade. It is however, the form of *wallichianum* known as 'Buxton's variety', that should be in every garden.

Discovered by the late Mr. Charles Buxton in his garden in Wales, and, of course, named after him, it became popular as soon as distributed; in fact, it received from the R.H.S. an Award of Garden Merit, as long ago as 1925. It can be said to have superseded *wallichianum* itself, and no wonder, for it produces cup-shaped flowers of a light yet rich blue, with a showy pure white central ring. It likes a cool but sunny place, and will grow in almost any soil provided it is well drained. It can easily be kept within bounds and freely produces its blooms from June until late autumn. Fortunately it comes true from seed, which is a great point in its favour, seeing that so many others do not.

Other quite good but little known hardy Geraniums include *G. pyrenaicum*, the Mountain Granesbill, with well-divided hairy leaves and reddish-mauve flowers. *G. versicolor,* the pencilled geranium, having pale pink flowers well veined with red; and *G. nodosum*, very similar to the previous species but with red flowers and smooth stems. Apart from *G. robertianum*, already mentioned, there are several other good biennial sorts, often found growing in rough places. Among these are, *G. molle*, the Dove's Foot Cranesbill, usually regarded as a weed; *columbianum*, with straggly growth, and rose-pink flowers; and *G. dissectum*, the jagged-leaved cranesbill, with much branched stems and divided foliage.

Among more recently introduced sorts is *G.* × *splendens* which apparently is a hybrid of *G. subcaulescens* and some other species. *G. balderina* is believed to be the result of a cross between *G. cinereum* and *subcaulescens*.

Also worthy of mention, is the little known or grown North American hardy species, *Geranium erianthum*. This is a native of coastal districts of British Columbia where it produces, from late April onwards, pale lavender flowers, the petals being pencil-marked a bright reddish-violet. Easy to grow in the sheltered rock and scree garden, it is also a delightful plant for the alpine house.

137

G. incisum from Southern California, is stronger growing and while being nothing special, makes a good plant for the front of the border. Attaining a height of 12 to 18 inches, the stems carry really large, deep rose-pink flowers, finely pencil-marked with crimson, both stems and leaves being quite hirsute. It is possible to find a number of colour variations from self-sown seedlings, some of which are not of a particularly desirable shade of colour. To maintain a true stock, it is essential to propagate by division, although this is not too easy because of the shape of the roots.

Seed of some of the hardy species is often available and it can be sown about $\frac{1}{2}$ inch deep in ordinary soil in a sunny position, out of doors, during April or in shallow boxes or pans of sandy soil in the cold frame or greenhouse. Subsequently, the seedlings are thinned out in the usual way and when of good size, can be moved to their flowering quarters.

The hardy geraniums are truly perennial, really practical plants which increase naturally without the necessity for division. It is quite easy in most cases to break off suitable pieces which can be planted in ordinary soil where they will root without any trouble. There are many hardy geraniums which make dense growth near the soil, thus forming a canopy of leaves. These act splendidly as a ground cover through which few weeds can penetrate.

The majority of these hardy species will grow well in either acid or limey soil, so long as it is reasonably well drained, and in fairly good condition, and they will flourish in both sun and partial shade. Whether used as a ground cover, or in the wild garden, hardy geraniums can be allowed to seed themselves and grow luxuriantly.

One of the best for this purpose is *G. pratense*, our native Meadow Cranesbill. This has forms in several shades of blue, as well as white, and beautifully cut foliage. The one drawback of growing this species and its varieties is that as in the case of nearly all geraniums, the seed pods when ripe, are liable to explode and send their seeds some distance away. This means that often, geranium plants may be found coming up in various parts of the garden where they are unwanted, and unless they are moved whilst young, the seedlings form thong-like roots which are not always easy to extract.

There are several double forms of *G. pratense* which seldom produce seeds, and they are therefore very suitable for growing fairly near the border. The advantage of *pratense* as a ground cover plant is that its basal leaves form in a large circle around the slowly increasing root-stock and in so doing, keeping the ground cool and weed free.

The Wood Cranesbill, *G. sylvaticum*, is also good for covering ground and seems to be able to withstand much more direct sun than many other species. The flowers are very freely produced from May onwards, the colour being lilac-blue or pinkish-blue contrasting with the foliage.

The Dusky Cranesbill, sometimes known as the Mourning Widow, is *G. phaeum*. In this, the petals are inclined to reflex as opposed to the wide open, upright flowers of the other species. They appear on stems of about 2 feet high, being a brownish-mauve, sometimes almost maroon shade. *G. phaeum* is an excellent ground covering plant since it forms a dense mat of divided leaves up to 9 inches high. Whilst not a plant for prominent positions, it is excellent for odd corners, among shrubs, and it keeps its foliage throughout the year.

Another very pleasing hardy species, which is aromatic to the touch, is *G. macrorrhizum*. This has rather creeping stems which root as they travel along the ground. It is a first-class subject for semi-shaded positions, although it does well in the sun, where however it remains more compact.

The much divided leaves form a really close dense ground cover and the heads of pretty pink flowers make it doubly attractive. If the leaves are lightly rubbed they emit a most pleasing fragrance. There are several forms of this, including *album*, white, and 'Ingwersen's Variety', lovely lilac-pink, both worth growing for their ground cover value as well as for the beauty of their flowers.

G. ibericum, a native of the Caucasus, which includes the ancient country of Iberia, is another splendid species. It has a number of good forms, one of the best being *platypetalum*, sometimes listed as a separate species. These two make fine plants for ground covering, their handsome divided, dark green downy leaves spreading out in all directions from the rootstock which, however, increases slowly.

Once established, the whole plant becomes entirely covered with violet-blue flowers which are veined and paler toward the centre. After the flowers have passed over, the foliage takes on a number of delightful Autumn tints. *G. ibericum*, and its forms are ideal for using in the front of sunny shrub borders, as well as for growing in partial shade.

G. grandiflorum is another first-class sort with deep blue flowers. This has rather more ferny, divided leaves and the flowers are veined crimson, and made more noticeable by the black stamens. It has several shorter forms, including the one known as *alpinum* or Gravetye. The flowers appear from May until well into the autumn, and always attract a good deal of attention.

Established plants can be readily divided into a number of single shoots, which soon develop into strong flowering plants. There is therefore, no reason at all why these hardy geraniums should not be used as an attractive ground cover, and for weed smothering. In addition to their value in these respects, they are most showy both in regard to their flowers and foliage.

Geranium carolinum, from North America, produces erect stems of up to 18 inches high with deeply divided leaves and clusters of pale magenta flowers, up to $\frac{1}{4}$ inch in diameter. This little plant is very suitable for the wild garden.

G. lowei from Madeira also has large divided leaves which colour up well in the autumn, the rose-coloured flowers containing a paler marked centre.

G. Wilfordii from Manchuria produces white flowers which are prettily striped rose, $\frac{1}{2}$ inch in diameter, and which show up well amongst the deeply cut foliage.

One of the values of these little plants is that they stand up well to both wind and rain and may therefore be used in exposed places as well as in the border, so long as their growth is restricted.

They do well in poor sandy soil and like both sun and partial shade. Seeds are sown in May or June, the plants being moved to their flowering positions in September. Alternatively, they can be sown into their flowering positions so long as the seedlings are well thinned out before they become very large.

Erodiums

Although *Erodium cicutaricum* is often overlooked, or intentionally ignored because it is one of our annual native wild flowers, it nevertheless produces the most charming and graceful little blossoms.

Whether one considers the attractive and ornamental foliage, the colour and form of the blooms, or the quaint, rigid, beak-like seed pods, all are equally desirable. It is normally to be found growing either on waste ground, where it seems able to resist drought, or quite frequently among cultivated field crops, where it flowers throughout the summer.

Of semi-upright habit the stems themselves are usually 9 to 12 inches long, although the tops may be only 6 or 7 inches from the ground, owing to their habit of growth. The pink flowers are divided into five parts, each one having a sepal, petal, stigma, and two stamens, one of which is sterile and rudimentary. Both the pinnate leaves and stems are hairy.

The derivation of the word *cicutaricum* is of much interest, since it comes from Cicula, a classical, but not the scientific, name for hemlock, and was given from the supposed likeness between the leaves of the two plants. Cicula is said to have been so named by Theophrastus, and indicates in the Greek, a top or cone, presumably referring to the connection between the whirling motion of a top and the giddiness which came upon anyone who was foolish enough to allow themselves to taste the poisonous Hemlock.

There are other species, and *E. moschatum* or the Musky Heronsbill is considerably larger growing, the flowers being bluish-purple while the less divided leaves emit a musk-like scent which of course, is indicated by the name.

E. maritimum is the Sea Heronsbill, sometimes found growing near the seashore. It is, however, a very small growing plant, with purple flowers and hairy stems and foliage. In some respects the cultivated erodiums may be said to be first-class examples of the geranium family, although some of them shed their petals so quickly that the plants must be frequently looked at to ensure the blooms are not missed.

In all cases the erodium flowers are followed by really large Heronsbill seed pods, which when ripe, have a habit of contracting to form a spiral, just as a ripe Sweet Pea pod behaves when it bursts. As the pointed seed, which has stiff hairs all sloping one way, are ejected, when the pods split and twist, they shoot upwards and forwards, like an arrow and as they fall, easily penetrate into the soil where they germinate.

Erodiums are chiefly natives of North Africa and Europe; practically all species emit some kind of smell when the foliage is bruised, in some cases this being not altogether pleasant. The erodiums make first-class plants for the rock garden, and are specially valuable in that when established, they have the ability to thrive in a dry or sandy soil, where many other subjects will not do well.

They look well growing in the crevices of a sunny wall, and have the capacity of producing blooms throughout the summer months. There are many species, some of which are very similar, and others which are hard to obtain. Taking some of the best alphabetically: *E. chamaedrioides roseum* produces, throughout the summer, a regular show of deep pink flowers, well set among glossy green leaves.

E. chrysanthum, is undoubtedly one of the loveliest, making little clumps of ferny, silvery-green foliage, from which arises attractive little sprays of yellow flowers.

E. corsicum is a little later, the freely borne small pink flowers coming on 4-inch stems, surrounded by clusters of grey foliage.

E. hymenodes has flushed pink petals, of which the upper ones have a reddish-brown spot at the base. Growing 10 to 12 inches high, the flowers appear from June until the early frosts come. This species is sometimes referred to as *E. trilobatum*.

E. macradenum is violet with flesh-pink and purple markings, and grows about 6 inches high.

E. manescavii is a native of the Pyrenees, and may be regarded as one of the very best. Growing quite large–and there are one or two forms which will develop to 18 inches or more in diameter–the fern-like leaves provide an excellent foil for the purplish-red, almost magenta blooms, which go on from May until September. If carefully placed where the flowers are not likely to clash with the colour of other subjects, they are quite effective.

E. pelargoniflorum, growing about 1 foot high, is not unlike *E. hymenodes*, excepting perhaps, that the petals have light purplish spots on them, while the sepals have a little tail coming from their points, which is not the case with the latter species. Both seed themselves freely, so that it is really best to keep up a supply of young plants, rather than attempt to retain the older plants, which so often, are either killed or damaged during the winter.

E. romanum commences to flower in the spring and often goes on showing colour until late autumn. Known in this country for well over 200 years, the purplish flowers appear on 6- to 9-inch stems.

G. incanus. A native of South Africa this appears to have more than one form. The leaves are finely cut, silky and silvery on the undersides. The white or pink handsome flowers appear in the dwarf form on 2 to 3 inch stems or in the taller types, on stems of 18 inches or more.

G. lucidum. An annual variety sometimes found growing wild in Northern counties. It forms rosettes of glossy leaves, the pinkish flowers being quite tiny and on reddish stems. The leaves colour beautifully in the autumn.

G. maderense. Named after the island of Madeira where it is known only in one locality. Of recent discovery, it is reckoned to be related to *G. palmatum*, differing in its tall stems, larger inflorescence and brown petioles. The petals are purplish-pink. Not yet offered by nurserymen it seems likely to become a useful greenhouse plant. Outdoors, it needs a warm sheltered position.

G. traversii. Known as the Chatham Island geranium, it is the form known as Russell Pritchard which is particularly fine. This has magenta-pink flowers produced over a carpet of grey-green leaves and which appear from June right until the autumn. It flourishes in sun and well drained soil and seen growing among grey foliaged plants is particularly attractive.

17 Some Geranium diseases

THE TWO commonest diseases of the geranium are grey mould and black leg. Technically the former is known as *Botrytis cinerea* whilst the latter is *Pythium de baryanum*. The former will also attack many types of ornamental plants and is particularly troublesome under cool, moist conditions. Botrytis thrives on decaying matter and this is why plant debris should not be left lying on the soil or in the greenhouse surrounds for they give rise to botrytis which will often spread rapidly to healthy plants.

This disease attacks leaves and stems of both mature and young plants. Sometimes it causes them to collapse quite quickly, on other occasions the disease works slowly and a certain amount of growth is made. Brown areas appear on the leaves and stem; the petals become discoloured and the flowers eventually wilt and fall. Later tiny spores of fungus are produced in very large quantities and these are seen as greyish fur appearing on the stems and leaves of affected plants. Provided the plants are grown under healthy, clean conditions, this disease should not cause any serious trouble.

There are various fungicide dusts which have been compounded specially for use against this disease and one of the most useful is Folosan. This is powerful enough to prevent disease spores from forming which in turn stops the spread of the disease, causing the affected parts to dry up. It is of course, important to begin the Folosan or similar treatment early in the season, so that the fungus does not build up. For this reason, some growers give a routine dusting at ten-day intervals from November onwards.

As botrytis thrives on plant debris in the soil a cloud method of dusting gives the most satisfactory results. Folosan and any similar powder should be blown into the air just above plant level, using a bellow type of duster and the fine powder will then settle on both plants and soil, so that no position of the staging or ground space is left untreated.

This thorough treatment is advisable, although it is permissible to simply dust the plants themselves. Experience has shown however, that sometimes the disease does start under the bench, so that if the powder reaches that position, the disease will be arrested before it gains a hold.

During recent years, much interest has been caused, particularly in the United States of America, regarding verticillium infection. This disease can easily be confused with bacterial disease and can prove quite destructive if not dealt with in the early stages of attack. It appears to have been first reported from several parts of the United States in 1940, and since then it has cropped up in different areas.

Some Geranium diseases

Not only are geraniums attacked but many kinds of nursery stock including herbaceous plants, shrubs and trees and even dahlias. It is in fact believed that dahlias carry the disease fungus in their tubers and it is because of this, that the disease has now become fairly widespread. It is perhaps best known as the cause of wilt in potatoes, tomatoes and other subjects.

Unfortunately, verticillium is a soil fungus and enters the plants through the roots. Since it forms tiny, hard sclerotic bodies, these help the fungus to survive and resist adverse conditions.

The disease affects geraniums in various ways and these are clearly indicated in a paper by Dr. Frank McWhorter which has been distributed by the Southern California Geranium Gardens of Gardena, California. We follow their list of symptoms, the first of which is dwarfing.

This is often noticed in plants while they are quite small. Cuttings from infected specimens, even though other plants in the same batch appear healthy, may grow slowly, form short internodes and bear leaves which are smaller than normal, although they are not usually discoloured in any way. The plants never attain a good size and look generally poor, which condition is often blamed on to the supplier.

Yellow spotting and the yellowing of the entire leaves is another symptom and this is often seen when stock plants, either indoors or open ground planted are examined. If this is noticed one should certainly suspect verticillium. The symptoms are first seen as bright yellow spots which gradually increase in size until the whole leaf becomes yellow. The yellowing caused by verticillium is noticeable by the fact that it is the clusters of upper leaves which become discoloured and not the lower foliage.

Whilst at first the coloration is bright yellow, it often becomes much duller and the danger here is that sometimes the spotting, at first caused by verticillium, is followed by botrytis disease. The yellow leaves drop prematurely and after a time, affected branches appear as short, pointed stubs.

Stem necrosis or die-back is also fairly prevalent and this is seen as bright yellow spotting of the leaves followed by necrosis of the stem terminals which gradually progresses several inches down the stems. In this case however, there is some resemblance between stem rot of the bacterial disease and verticillium. Initial necrosis due to verticillium is frequently noticed by sudden dying and intense blackening of the young florescence.

An unusual feature of stem rot is the fact that within the stem at the base of the rot, the plant forms a corky cambium layer that separates the dead tissues from the living. The terminals are killed and form no more foliage. In this way the disease differs from bacterial blight. In the latter case, the blighted stems frequently recover and continue to grow.

The wilting of geranium foliage is also brought about by verticillium infection; in fact, this is the condition which is often referred to by growers simply as wilt. Plants growing in gardens do not always wilt badly but the foliage simply appears to fold downwards during the warmer part of the day. The plants grow slowly and seem generally sluggish.

It is the *Pelargonium hortorum* cultivars which seem susceptible to this disease and it is only very rarely that *P. domesticum* and the scented-leaved types devlop wilt, although sometimes they do exhibit bright yellow, spotted foliage and become somewhat dwarfed in habit. The older leaves on the ivy-leaved forms are sometimes affected, in which case there is little or no coloration. Instead, the foliage turns an ash-brown colour making the plants quite unsightly.

It does seem as though the most likely source of infection is from outdoor soil in which stock plants are grown. There seems to be more risk of this if geraniums follow dahlias or other composites. It has been reported from Oregon that one outbreak in garden plantings was traced to a stock which had come from soil where potatoes had previously been grown. These potatoes had made poor growth and subsequently wilted and died, such symptoms being typical of verticillium diseased potatoes.

There are of course, a number of specialist geranium growers in Southern California and these firms take every care to ensure that the stocks they propagate are of the very finest quality. Anything that we have said in regard to disease prevalence in the United States should not be taken to infer that there is carelessness in propagation or in the stock used. It has long been the practice of these growers to take particular care in the growing and propagation of geraniums and they always make a point of selecting, as far as is possible, virus-free stock plants.

The plants are grown for two or more generations in sterilized soil and it is a practice of many firms to subject the cuttings to culture tests to ensure that they are not in any way affected by bacteria. While bacterial infection of geraniums is the same disease everywhere, it can be spread from only one geranium to another. On the other hand, verticillium is particularly insidious because there are hundreds of host plants, all of which can transmit the disease to geraniums plants to which it is fatal.

Bacterial stem rot has been known for well over 70 years and is caused by a species of bacteria named *Xanthomonas pelargonii*. The bacteria attacks the leaves, stems and cuttings of *P. hortorum* and is sometimes responsible for quite heavy losses to commercial growers of geraniums. The ivy-leaved geraniums are also affected but *Pelargonium domesticum* is resistant to the disease.

The symptoms as generally found on *P. hortorum* cultivars are as follows: very small water-soaked areas appear on the undersides of the leaf and occasionally on the upper surface too. The spots enlarge and become more conspicuous. After a few days, a water-soaked area may be formed around the edges of the spot in the shape of a halo. Within several days the spot becomes brown, sunken and dry and if there are many spots on a leaf the whole area becomes yellow and withers and subsequently drops from the plant.

The bacteria does not always migrate from infected leaves to the stem but in some instances it rapidly progresses, usually via the petiole, from the leaf downwards into the stem and then causes the stem to rot. This calls for regular examination.

Varieties vary considerably in their resistance or immunity to the disease. In some cases there is no leaf spot stage of the disease, but there is a wilting at the edges, and the whole leaf dies in about a couple of weeks after the first symptoms are noticed. Growers usually take this to be a preliminary to stem rot.

Sterilized soil seems to be the answer where soil troubles have been encountered, although of course, healthy growing conditions should always be maintained, and it is these more than anything else, which will sustain clean stocks.

Some Geranium diseases

Virus diseases have become very prominent during recent years, and they can do much damage to geraniums. Once they gain a hold, they can easily ruin a whole stock. Any suspicious looking plants should be destroyed. Virus is seen in a number of ways, since there appears to be many types. The one known as 'crinkle leaf' is characterized by irregular or sometimes round, yellow or white spots, and usually the leaves are ruffled, are dwarfed, sometimes being malformed as well.

Then there is the light and dark mottling of the leaves, and also the dwarfing of plants, an indication that mosaic disease is present. This must not be confused with a similar condition brought about by nutritional imbalance. Aphides of various kinds are often responsible for the spread of virus diseases.

Geranium rust, *Puccinia pelargonii zonalis*, has become troublesome in Britain during the last ten years. It shows first as rusty-looking pustules on the undersides of leaves. Affected plants begin to look sickly for as the fungus develops within the leaf tissues, the surface ruptures setting free more spores, thus repeating the process.

In the greenhouse or frame, avoid a heavily humid atmosphere and never allow roots to become waterlogged. Pelargoniums are natives of warm, drier areas where rust does not occur. Spores are distributed by wind, rain or water splashings. They can overwinter on old leaves and the disease can be carried over from one season to another.

Sulphur sprays give some control so long as all parts of the plants are contacted or a dusting of 10 per cent Zineb powder, often distributed under the name of Hexyl Plus or Dithane, if used regularly, usually prevents the trouble spreading provided all parts of the foliage are reached. Never propagate from plants even suspected of being affected. Do not bring stools of infected Zonals into the greenhouse in the autumn.

The incubation period of the spores is 10 to 14 days and attacks seem most likely when the temperature is around 50 deg., F. Experiments show that the spores can be killed if held in a temperature of 100 deg., F. (37·5 C.) at a relative humidity of 80 to 90 per cent., which may not always be possible for the amateur gardener to provide. Ivy-leaved varieties are rarely attacked, probably due to their harder skins.

Apart from actual diseases, there are several physiological troubles, many of which originate from faulty root conditions, unfavourable weather or poor culture. One of the most common is known as oedema or dropsy. This is most likely to occur in warm greenhouses or in places where plants are crowded together. All affected specimens become spotted, then rusty looking, and corky. The remedy is to provide plenty of air and light and not to overwater. Marginal discoloration of the leaves is usually due to potash deficiency, whilst anaemic looking leaves can often be improved by applying weak solutions of nitrogen. Very often the leaves take on a reddish or other bright coloured appearance. This is not necessarily a sign of disease but is caused by low atmospheric or soil temperatures. As a rule, correction of faulty environment will restore the plants to normal health.

It sometimes happens that plants make lanky growth, with little foliage, and this is usually the result of overcrowding, and insufficient light. The remedy therefore is to provide better conditions, although there are some varieties which are naturally taller growing than others. It is never wise to propagate from plants which show unusually tall stems with widely spaced joints.

Sometimes the lower leaves of geraniums become discoloured, particularly during the autumn months. This may suggest that some disease is present, but very often it is simply a question of cold and old age, for it is a fact that almost all pelargoniums (geraniums) are half hardy and consequently need rest, which usually results in some basal leaf shedding and the high coloration of other fully matured leaves.

Some varieties are much more prone to this condition than others. 'Jewel' for instance, will go almost crimson at certain stages. Many, perhaps the majority of, people hear that geraniums are happy at a temperature around 40 degrees F. This is probably so, if such a heat were constant, but so often the temperature is allowed to drop to almost freezing point so that it is no wonder that plants under these conditions want to rest.

Another observation worth making is that constant use of insecticides tends to cause leaf yellowing. Then another speedy cause of trouble is paraffin stove fumes. Geraniums most definitely do not like these.

In the case of insect infestations, there are usually bodies or eggs present and many people use some of the modern sprays regardless of whether they are specifically for geraniums. It is really appalling when one considers the treatment that is often meted out to geraniums, and it is not therefore surprising that they sometimes behave in a peculiar way.

Leafy gall is the name given to the disorder which produces cauliflower-like growths on pelargoniums at ground level, and affected plants cease to develop normally. This trouble is reckoned to be brought about by bacterial action, which is shown in various forms, and is sometimes responsible for the condition known as fasciation.

The method of attack varies, but usually a gall varying from the size of a pea to the size of a marble is found growing at soil level from the main stem. Affected plants seem to stand still, although they rarely die. There is still some mystery of the cause of the working of the gall formation, although it is due to Corynebacteriam fascians.

It is possible that the bacteria feeds on something carried in the sap stream of the host plant. At the moment, there is no cure and it is wise as soon as the symptoms are seen, to destroy the plants by burning together with the soil around the roots. Cuttings should not be taken from such plants, although up to the present there is no actual evidence that leaf gall is transmitted from affected plants.

Leaves sometimes flag or droop on bright sunny days. This occurs, particularly with plants having soft, lush foliage. Such specimens transpire more moisture than the roots can obtain, resulting in the foliage and sometimes the stems too, becoming soft and flaccid.

Plants grown under cool conditions from their earliest stages are less likely to be affected. Some growers make a practice of spraying young plants overhead with cold water from the early spring onwards. This enables them to withstand sharp changes in temperature.

I am much indebted to Mr. F. A. Bode, Junior, and former Editor of *Geraniums Around the World*, for permission to quote an article which appeared in that publication some years ago, regarding bullhead deformities.

'The following notes are observations made during several years' study of the condition. No concrete proofs can be offered, so like all such studies the resulting theories are simply organized logic which in some future time may

Some Geranium diseases

be proved to be correct: (1) Organic disease caused by virus or mosaic, although this seems least likely. (2) Induced mutation by chemical imbalance of soil, air or water; or very possibly chemical or physical damage to the auxiliary bud while still minute. (3) Hereditary mutation. This seems the most probable according to the conclusions drawn from observing hundreds of thousands of stock plants, as well as from such physical studies as removing affected portions of plants and then blinding certain buds in an effort to determine the exact location of bullhead growth.

'The bullhead (sometimes called bullet-head or simply bullets) appears as a deformity of zonal geraniums (*P. hortorum*). This deformity is characterized by heavy stiff flower stems and extra long pedicels (floret stems) which are stiffly upright. The floret is borne squarely at the top of the pedicel and may or may not be deformed, depending upon the hardness of the sepals. These sepals usually give way to the opening floret by bending away at the base of the bud, but keeping their cupped in-bud shape. Fewer than the usual number of florets are typical.

'The plant of the true bullhead is always stronger than an unaffected plant, and it commonly makes a plant about half again the size of a normal plant. The stemwood is large and the foliage coarse in texture and appearance.

'For some time the bullhead has been regarded by many as a disease of the virus or mosaic type; and although I certainly do not entirely eliminate this possibility, I do feel that obvious indications point directly to a natural mutaton which, if our history of the geranium family were better known, might be traced to an incompatible ancestor.

'With only an occasional variance, bullheads are found entirely within certain cultivar families which sport or mutate readily. Cultivars most commonly afflicted in the United States are 'Magenta Ruby' and the blood strain varieties 'Better Times', 'Royal Times', 'Edna', 'Pink Better Times', 'Galli-Curci', and several other offspring; the Fiat family including 'Pink Fiat', 'Fiat Enchantress', 'Fiat Supreme' and a multitude of other sports ('Red Fiat' is not a blood member of this group and is not affected); the 'La Fiesta'-'Kovalevski'-'Cuba' group, and the 'Irvington Beauty' family. This list also includes the greatest source of plant-sport parents and although the cultivars listed are very popular varieties, yet they actually comprise a very small portion of the total number of blood lines.

'One family of cultivars which should be included in the above group, but which has been saved to use as an example of the theory, is the one which includes 'Double New Life'. 'Double New Life' is a sport of the variety 'Vesuvius', which first sported to the semi-double scarlet 'Wonderful'. Then sometime before 1876, 'Vesuvius' sported to our present-day 'Single New Life' a white striped scarlet novelty. Later, 'Single New Life' sported to a salmon 'Single New Life' and a salmon-lake variety. In June 1878, the announcement was published that a Mr. Knight of Battle had a sport of 'Wonderful' similar to 'Single New Life' with its striped scarlet petals but the flowers were very double and quite small. This is our present-day 'Double New Life' ('Star and Stripes', 'Peppermint Stick', 'Flag of Denmark') and it is the most mutated of the group. Of the four or five cultivars of this family which we still grow, Double New Life is the only one that is badly affected with bullheads. This very small and very double oddly striped flower which blooms profusely on a medium-small plant, is outstanding in the light of

147

mutations. Unfortunately, this plant readily mutates to bullheads. The bull-head form develops hundreds of flower stems and buds which refuse to open, and the plant becomes very strong and nearly double the size of its flowering parent.

'Practically all plant sports of geraniums appear in the heavy side shoots emanating from the base of the plant outward. Seldom are sports found on top growth or on shoots that appear from within the plant and originate above the main point of branching.

'Good flowering wood never changes to bullheads. If cuttings are taken from upper wood or from side wood with well-developed flowers, no bullhead plants result. However, it is not always possible to differentiate between the good and bad during winter when there are no flowers, or when young growth is taken before flowers develop. It is natural to take strong cuttings from newly made side growth, and in the case of 'Better Times', this can result in upwards of 15 per cent bullheads.

Putting this knowledge into actual practice by choosing the proper wood and flowering the rooted cuttings before field planting, we find that we rogue less than 1 per cent. Yet, it is necessary to occasionally rogue out a few plants developing bullhead side branches, in order to avoid the possibility of creating several bullhead plants from a single mutated branch. Also, by this constant roguing, the variety strains are losing their propensity for mutating to bull-heads. Like so many so-called diseases, there are two sets of almost identical symptoms for two very different types of bullheads: (1) The above de-scribed symptoms for the mutative-type of bullheads and (2) A second much less difficult to control form which is nothing more than deformed florets caused by the presence of two-spotted mites which lay their eggs in the flower buds when the buds are very small. This causes a crippling effect to the floret. Many of the buds never develop due to injury; this in turn duplicates another symptom of the mutative bullhead, that of fewer florets to the flower head.

'To differentiate between the two, the grower need only observe that the plant of the mite-type bullhead is of normal growth, or even stunted if the infestation is very severe. Inspection of the ready-to-open bud, will usually show a tiny hole through the petals, and the floret will open as from a whorl; that is, the inner edges of the petals are furled in a long pointed bud, while the outer edges in their effort to unfurl, radiate stiffly outward rather than opening outward and downward.

'Occasionally, a plant will produce extra peduncles out of the top of the flower truss. This is something which also happens with a number of other ornamental plants and also with the double bedding daisies and calendulas. It is usually referred to as "hen and chickens". With most plants these out-growths are of normally shaped flowers.

'Some geraniums however, notably the New Life varieties, do not produce normal flowers at all, but simply a continuation of sepals and petals irregularly placed. This sometimes produces a spikey effect. This abnormality rarely occurs in the Ivy-leaved or Regal varieties and I have never seen the Zonal pelargoniums affected in this way.

'The cause of this abnormality is uncertain, although there is no doubt that to some extent it is a seasonal happening, related to local conditions.'

18 Pests and their treatment

GERANIUMS are not particularly susceptible or prone to pest attacks; in fact, grown under good clean healthy conditions, it is really surprising how free from troubles these plants are. This applies in particular to the zonal varieties. The regals and scented-leaf types seem more likely to be affected but attacks when they do occur, are of a mild nature and if dealt with before they gain a real hold, they do not present any undue difficulties.

Very often geraniums of all types are grown in greenhouses where there is quite a wide range of other subjects, and if these become affected, as they often do, the pests are liable to settle on the geraniums too. It is therefore necessary to be well informed as to the possibilities and to have such information as will enable one to identify and deal with the pests by the best possible means.

Insect pests vary in their method of attack and because of this, they may need to be tackled in different ways, which may be in the egg, larvae or adult stages. As will be readily understood, there is no single insecticide that is likely to be effective in all cases.

Insects can be divided into two main groups. The first includes those which bite or chew and this means earwigs, wood-lice, caterpillars of various moths, butterflies, sawflies and cockroaches. The second group takes in thrips, mealy bug, capsid bugs and aphides. The latter is almost a group in itself, since there are so many types and they are particularly troublesome, for not only do they spoil growth, by their sucking activities, but through their saliva, they carry viruses which rapidly spread through the plant.

The vine weevil will sometimes attack geraniums, especially during the winter. This pest is like a small beetle, the larvae of which is sometimes imported into the greenhouse in the soil. These feed on the leaves and eventually emerges as little beetles, which can sometimes be seen on the leaves. The usual control is a Malathion spray in one of its modern forms, but these must be used with the greatest of care.

The root nematode or eelworm is rarely troublesome in this country, but when present, causes plants to look sickly, stunted and without vigour. Severe infestations may cause the plants to die. Badly attacked plants should be destroyed and fresh soil used for any new plants. This is one of the few occasions on which the use of steam sterilized soil may be an advantage.

Although there are black, red, grey and green aphides, it is the latter which are the most troublesome to the gardener, and they are usually referred to as greenfly. Unfortunately, some of them are very tiny and they are not always

149

noticed until they have become established on plants, so that it pays to look over one's stock from time to time, to ensure that greenfly is not there. They increase rapidly, and by their work cause the foliage to become curled and distorted. They spoil the growing points and their activities often lead to a discoloration or marking of the blooms.

Another undesirable feature of greenfly attack is the sticky honeydew which is excreted by aphides and this, in turn, encourages the development of a fungus known as sooty mould. Fortunately, this mould is not of a spreading type, and can soon be cleared if aphides are kept in check. The presence of aphides also encourages ants, which feed on the honey-dew. This is one of the reasons why ants too, should be kept from working near geraniums. Aphides have of course, many natural enemies, particularly ladybirds, hover-flies and lace-winged flies, whilst in the open ground, sparrows and other small birds feed on greenfly.

The range of present-day greenfly killers is extremely wide, so that it becomes almost puzzling for the average gardeners to know what to use. Nowadays, there are many quite strong sprays, some of a poisonous nature which are widely recommended, not only for ornamental but edible plants too. Whilst the majority of these certainly do the work for which they are intended, some also destroy the beneficial insects as well, including the predators such as ladybirds, which have been created to keep down the harmful pests. This means that if such insecticides are used, a vicious circle is formed, whereby it becomes necessary to continually spray and dust the plants because the natural balance of predators and pests has been broken. The continued use of insecticides cannot be wholeheartedly recommended, since these not only destroy pests but may also lead to the destruction of a number of useful insects.

What can one use on geraniums? Nicotine is certainly safe if used in moderation, and the brand known as Mortopal is a really good greenfly killer, if applied strictly in accordance with directions on the tin. The old-fashioned Quassia extract and soft soap is also effective, and safe. The best method, particularly if using Mortopal or any other insecticide wash, is to spray in the evening, being most careful to reach the undersides of the leaves and centres of the plant, and then cleanse the plants by spraying with clear water the following morning, thus avoiding the possibility of the flowers or foliage becoming discoloured.

Do this as soon as the first aphis is seen, and thus make eradication much easier. Make sure to spray any other plants in the same house, and also into any holes and crevices there may be in the greenhouse woodwork and walls. The fumigating of the greenhouse with nicotine or other shreds, is also effective, but here again it is essential to follow the manufacturers' instructions. At the present time, the so-called B.H.C. insecticides are widely used against aphis. These act as a contact insecticide, a stomach poison or a fumigant. One well-tried brand is Sybol, which is effective against a whole range of pests, besides aphids. The great advantage of Sybol is that it does not stain the foliage or flowers.

White fly will, on occasion, concentrate on the regal varieties, but rarely on the zonals. They are easy to detect when they are flying about or settling on the foliage, and this is another instance where speed is necessary in dealing with the pests, for they also increase very rapidly. Fumigation is a means of control and there are a number of special White Fly Killers, which, however, if wrongly used, may damage both flowers and foliage of geraniums as well as those of other plants. Here again, the makers' instructions must be followed in detail.

Sometimes caterpillars will eat the foliage of geraniums, and once damage is noticed, regular examination of the leaves is advisable so as to be able to destroy the eggs, which if left, will soon hatch out to bring another generation of caterpillars into being. Where convenient, shake the plants over newspaper in order to dislodge any of the pests. They can then easily be destroyed. The now rarely practised job of examining the plants at night under artificial light, will also prove most rewarding in revealing the caterpillars. Any of the good insecticides forcibly sprayed on to the plants, will usually prove effective in destroying the caterpillars.

Very occasionally, mealy bug and thrips will appear, but since they usually only do so as result of neglect and the accumulation of dirt, they are not likely to trouble the enthusiastic geranium grower, who will, as his normal routine, ensure that clean conditions and a buoyant atmosphere are provided for his treasures. With the former, fumigating with nicotine or the use of derris are usually effective, while with thrips, the use of Smoke 'bombs' will normally stamp out the pests which are more likely to appear in a hot, dry atmosphere.

Although red spider is not uncommon in greenhouses and conservatories, this is another pest which only thrives under close, dry conditions and since geraniums really prefer a rather moist atmosphere, there is rarely any trouble from this pest. Should it be suspected, extra moisture applied, not only as needed by the plants but also to the pots and standing places, will do much to prevent the geraniums being harmed. The spraying of the plants with pyrethrum powder, if applied to both sides of the foliage, will be effective in destroying the pests.

Woodlice will also sometimes damage geraniums, and since they are to be found almost everywhere both indoors and out, regular steps should be taken to keep them in check. All decaying wood and rubbish should be removed, and any other likely hiding place cleared away. The old-fashioned method of applying paraffin to the place where the woodlice are known to frequent will prove most helpful.

On very infrequent occasions black fly will settle on greenhouse geraniums, and these may be eradicated by the same means as recommended for white fly.

Some reliable suppliers of Pelargoniums and Geraniums

The following is a small selection of suppliers, arranged in alphabetical order, to serve as an introduction. In compiling such a list, it is easy to unintentionally omit some firms that should be included, but the selection that follows, though certainly not complete, does contain some of the leading growers and suppliers.

T. & M. Adkins, 310 Alcester Road South, Kings Heath, Birmingham,
Abermule Nurseries, Abermule, Montgomeryshire.
Ashfield Nurseries, Dunnington, York.
T. A. Bennett (Monica Bennett) Cypress Nursery, Blackheath, Birmingham.
Clifton Nurseries, Cherry Orchard Road, Chichester, Sussex.
J. W. Cole & Son, 16 Holdich Street, Peterborough.
East Lynne Gardens, Lamb Lane, Ponthir, Monmouthshire.
D. Gamble & Sons, Highfield Nurseries, Longford, Derbyshire.
Greybridge Geraniums, Fibrex Nurseries Ltd., Evesham, Worcs.
Harrison, The Gardens, Sutton Scarsdale, Nr. Chesterfield, Derbyshire.
D. & M. Jackson, Woodville Nurseries, Cragg Valley, Mytholmroyd, Yorks.
Morden Nurseries, 8A Edward Avenue, Wandle Road, Morden, Surrey.
R. W. Parfitt, Springfield Nursery, North Tuddenham, Norfolk.
F. G. Read, Woodhurst, Cucumber Lane, Brundall, N0R 86Z.
Telston Nurseries, Otford, Sevenoaks, Kent.
J. E. Thorp, 357 Finchhampstead Road, Wokingham, Berks.
Vicarage Farm Nursery, 256 Great West Road, Heston, Middlesex.
G. Wallwin, Grove Hall Nurseries, Grove, Retford, Notts.
Wyck Hill Geraniums, Stow on the Wold, Gloucestershire.
K. Hudson, 128 Craddocks Avenue, Ashtead, Surrey distributor for Morfs 'Margot' Australian Pelargoniums.
Guernsey Propagation Ltd., Les Effards, St. Sampsons, Guernsey, C. Isles distributors for Fischer Pelargoniums of West Germany.
The International Geranium Society, 711 Cole Avenue, Los Angeles, California, 90038 U.S.A.
The Canadian Geranium & Pelargonium Society, 105 Dolly Vardon Boulevard, Scarborough, 722, Ontario, Canada.
The South African Pelargonium & Geranium Society, 403 Fleming Hall, Koch Street, Johannesburg, S. Africa.

Mrs. E. Both, Geranium Nurseries, Adelaide, S. Australia.

Mrs. R. A. Gilson, 177 Fullers Road, Chatswood, N.S.W. 2067, Australia.

E. C. Smith, Dandenong Nurseries, 20 Maurice Street, Dandenong, Victoria, 3175.

Morfs Margot Nurseries, P.O. Box 89, Belmont, N.S.W., Australia.

The Windermere Floral Gardens, 333 Lock Street, Dunnville, Ontario, Canada.

Petersfield Nurseries, P.O. Box 101, Kroondal, Transvaal, S. Africa.

Merry Gardens, 1 Somerton Road, Camden, Main, U.S.A.

Wilson Bros., Roachdale, Indiana, U.S.A.

Oatland Gardens, 2130, Chestnut Everett, Washington 98201, U.S.A.

South California Geraniums, P.O. Box 121, Encinitas, California 92024.

J. N. Anderson & Sons, Wellesley Road, Nelson Crescent, Napier, New Zealand.

O. Wulliman, Jungpflanzen Kulturen, Grenchen, Switzerland.

Index

Aiton, 17, 18
Andrews, H. C., 16, 20
Aphides, 149–50
Asparagus spregeri, 58
Aucuba japonica, 94
Ayton, A. C., 131–2

Bacterial stem rot, 143–4
Baileyana, 20–1
Bentick, Mr., 17
Black fly, 151
Black leg, 43–4, 142
Black rot, 42
Bode, F. A., Jnr., 146–7
Botrytis disease, 142–3
Breiter, 20
British Geranium Society, 21, 24, 48, 54, 93, 110
British Pelargonium and Geranium Society, 21, 25, 26, 116
Bullhead deformity, 146–8
Buxton, Charles, 137

Caterpillars, 150–1
Cavanilles, 20; Works, '*Icones et Descriptiones Plantarum*', 20q.
Chlorophyll, 36, 94, 95
Cineraria maritima, 53
Com-Pel liquid feed, 117
Complon, Bishop, 18
'Crane's Bill' (Cranesbill), 15, 18, 133, 136–8
Crinkle leaf, 145
Cultivar families, 147–8
Cuttings, 41–9: success with, 44; method for rooting, 46–7

Delavay, Père, 134
Die-back, 143
Dillenius, 18; Works, *Hortus Elthamensis,* 18q.
Dioscorides, 15
Diseases, 142–8
Dithene, 145

Edelpelargonien, 19
Eelworm, 149
Eranium, 18: variety, 'Paul Crampel', 18
Erodium, 15–16, 18, 140–1; species of, 140–1

Farrer, Reginald, 134, 135
Florists Exchange, 44
Foliar feeding, 35
Forrest, George, 134

Geranium, 15–16: bedding-out, 51–5; Bird's Egg, 118; bottled, 65; Bruant types, 76; cactus-flowered, 118–19; carefree strains, 49–50; carnation-flowered, 120; culture of, 34–8; cuttings, 41–9
    method for rooting, 46–7; deacon, 117; difference between geraniums and pelargoniums, 16, 18; dwarf, 112–17
    cultivation of, 114, 116; flowering and care in winter, 130–2: genera of, 15–16; grafting, 47–9; Horseshoe, 67; hybrid, ivy-leaved, 91–2; in pots, 60–5; Irene strain, 69–70; ivy-leaved,

16, 18, 67, 77, 87–91; leaves of, uses for, 32; methods of propagation, 39–47; miniature, 67, 112; new life, 120; Phlox-eye, 121; popularity of, 15; propagation by leaf or leaf axil cuttings, 48–9; Rosebud, 25, 121; scented-leaf, 67, 105–11; species of, 133–41; stellar, 55

varieties of, 55; unique, 121–2; uses of, 26; variegated-leaved, 93–104; zonal, 16, 19, 21, 23, 45, 47, 54, 61, 67–9: varieties: 'A Happy Thought', 53, 96, 97, 100; 'Abel Carriere', 48, 89; 'A. T. Johnson', 134; 'A. M. Mayne', 52, 74; 'Beatrix Little', 55, 70; 'Black Douglas', 99; 'Black Vesuvius', 47, 53, 62, 112; 'Butterfly', 96; 'Caroline Schmidt', 25, 59, 70, 96–7, 131; 'Charles Turner', 58, 59, 89; 'Chelsea Gem', 59, 72, 97; 'Chocolate Flower', 136; 'Crystal Palace Gem', 53, 96, 97; 'Decorator', 52, 53, 54, 70, 131; 'Distinction', 99; 'Double Henry Jacob', 131; Fleuriste, 50; 'Flower of Spring', 25, 53, 96, 97; 'F. V. Raspail', 131; 'Galilee', 58, 89; 'Golden Crampel', 97; 'Golden Leaf Geranium', 97; 'Golden Harry Hieover', 97; 'Gustav Emich', 52, 54, 55, 58, 72; 'Harry Hieover', 25, 53; 'Hermine', 52; 'Ingwersen's Variety', 139; 'King of Denmark', 52, 58, 61, 72; 'Lady Churchill', 59, 97; 'Lady Plymouth', 97; 'Lady Warwick', 68, 74, 131; 'Lady Washington', 19, 77; 'L'Amour', 50; 'Lass O'Gowrie', 97; 'L'Elegante', 88; 'Little Trot', 97; 'Madame Crousse', 52; 'Madame Salleron', 97; 'Marechal McMahon', 97; 'Martha', 19, 77; 'Maxim Kovalevski', 52, 68, 75, 76; 'Mephistopheles', 99; 'Miss Burdett Coutts', 98; 'Mrs. G. Clark', 99; 'Mrs. H. Cox', 53, 97; 'Mrs. E. G. Hill', 52, 61, 73; 'Mrs. Kendall Clark', 136; 'Mrs. Lawrence', 52, 72, 76; 'Mrs. Mapping', 97; 'Mrs. Parker', 97; 'Mrs. Pollock', 53, 97; 'Mrs. Quilter', 53, 59, 62, 98; 'Mrs. Strang', 97; 'Nittany Lion', 49; 'Notting Hill Beauty', 52, 73, 131; 'One in a Ring', 99; 'Paul Crampel', 52, 54, 55, 58, 61, 65, 69, 72, 131; 'Pink Rambler', 25; 'Prince of Orange', 20; 'Queen of Denmark', 52, 73; 'Queen of the Whites', 131; 'Red Black Vesuvius', 98–9; 'Red Rambler', 25; 'Rose Clair', 134; 'Royal Purple', 52; 'Sailors Knot', 136; 'Salmon Black Vesuvius', 99, 112; 'Salmonia', 62; 'Sansovino', 68, 75; 'Silver Queen', 136; 'Sir Percy Blakeney', 59, 91; 'Skies of Italy', 63, 98; 'Sprinter', 50; 'The Speaker', 52, 73; 'Turtle's Surprise', 99; 'Vera Dillon', 55, 74; 'Verona', 97; 'Victory', 52; *Abutilon thompsonii*, 52; *g. capitatum*, 32; *g. citriodorum*, 20; *g. indicum noctu odoratum*, 16; *g. indicum odoratum flore maculato*, 16; *g. robertianum*, 18, 32, 133.

Geranium cakes, 32
Geranium punch, 33
Geranium, rose, rolls, 33
Geranium rust, 145
Geranoil, 32
Grafting, 47–9
Greenfly, 150
Greenhouse heating, 37
Grey mould, 142
Grieve, Peter, 93–4

Hanging baskets, 57–60
Harrison, Leonard, 48
Helxine solierolii, 59
Herb Robert, 18
Hermann, Paul, 17
'Heron's Bill' (Heronsbill), 15–16, 18, 140
Hexyl Plus, 145
Hudson, Mrs. K., 86

Insect pests, 149
Insecticides, use of, 146
International Code of Nomenclature for Cultivated Plants, 22
International Geranium Society, 33

Johnson, Thomas, 16; Works, *Gerard's Herball*, 16q.

Keeping young stock, 44

Leafy gall, 146
L'Heritier, 16
Linaria cymbalaria, 58
Linnaeus, 15–16; Works, *Species Plantarum*, 15q.
Lonicers aureo-reticulata, 94

Martius, 20; Works, '*Plantarum Horti Academici Erlangensis*', 20q.
McWhorter, Dr. Frank, 143
Mealy bug, 151
Moisture requirements, 37
Monograph of the Genus Geranium, 20
Moore, Harold E., Jnr., 20

Nichols, Beverley, 24; Works, *Laughter on the Stairs*, 24q.
Nicotine, 150, 151

Oedema or dropsy, 145
Organic liquid fertilizers, 35

Paraffin burners, use of, 37–8
Parkinson, 17
Pelargoniums, 15–16: angel, 22; carnation, 23; difference between pelargoniums and geraniums, 16, 18; dwarf, 29; fragility of, 37; groups of species, 21; hybrid ivy-leaved, 21, 29, 91–2; ivy-leaved, 21, 25, 29; judging of, notes on, 28–30; liking for water, 45; miniature, 29; popularity of, 45; primary hybrids, 22; raising from seed, 49–50; scented-leaved, 21, 25, 29; seedlings, labelling of, 29; Show or Regal, 19, 21, 25, 26, 67, 77–80, 81–6; species, 22, 67, 124–9; standards, 29; tuberous-rooted, 122–3; unique, 21; uses of, 26–7; uses for making bouquets as healing agents, etc., leaves of, 27–8, 32; zonal, 21, 25, 26, 51, 70, 72–6, 93, 130; varieties; 'Burgundy', 80–1; 'California Brilliant', 111; 'Caprice', 81; 'Carisbrooke', 80, 81; 'Clorinda', 107, 111; 'Grand Slam', 80; 'Jean',

21; 'Lord Bute', 81; 'Mrs. Kingsley', 111; 'Rhodomine', 81; 'Rollinson's Unique', 111; 'Skelly's Pride', 21, 62; *p. acerifolium*, 20; *p. acerifolium L'Heritier ex Aiton*, 21; *p. angulosum*, 77; *p. capitatum*, 110, 126; *p. citriodorum*, 20; *p. citriodorum (Cavanilles) Martius*, 20–1; *p. citriodorum Schrank*, 21; *p. citrosum Voigt*, 20; *p. x citrosum*, 20; *p. x citrosum Voigt*, 20; *p. x citrosum Voigt ex Sprague*, 21; *p. crispum*, 20; *p. crispum variegatum*, 97; *p. cucullatum*, 17, 77; *p. domesticum*, 19, 77, 111, 132, 143, 144; *p. x dumosum*, 122; *p. fragrans*, 110; *p. fulgidum*, 121; *p. grandiflorum*, 77; *p. graveolens*, 107, 111, 126; *p. hederaefolium*, 88; *p. hortorum*, 67, 91, 143, 144, 147; *p. inquinans*, 18, 67, 76, 124, 125; *p. odoratissium*, 110; *p. parviflorum*, 110; *p. peltatum*, 18, 19, 88, 91; *p. radula*, 110; *p. terebinthaceum*, 110; *p. tomentosum*, 108; *p. triste*, 16, 17, 127; *p. zonale*, 18, 19, 67, 76, 124, 128, 132
Pests and treatment of, 149–51
Phosfon, 64
Pollination, 39–41

Quassia extract, 150

Read, F. G., 116
Red spider, 151
Root nematode, 149

Schrank, 20; Works, *Sylloge Plantarum Novarum*, 20q.
Seed boxes, use of for cuttings, 43
Shading for geraniums, 36
Sowing seed, 41
Sprague, Thomas, 20
Spry, Mrs. Constance, 25; Works, *How to do the Flowers*, 25q.
Stem necrosis, 143
Sticky honeydew, 150
'Stork's Bill' (Storksbill), 15–16, 18, 41
Stringer, Rev. S. P., 117
Styles, D. J., 110; Works, *The Oil of Geranium*, 110q.

Index

Sweet, R., 23; Works, *Geraniaceae,*
 23q.
Sybol, 150

Temperature, importance of, 36
Thrips, 151
Tradescant, John, 16–17, 127
Tradescantia, 58

Urns and tubs, use of for growing
 geraniums, 63–4

Van der Stel, Willem Adriaan, 18
Verbena venosa, 53

Verticillum infection, 142–4
Vine weevil, 149

White fly, 150–1
Window boxes, 56–7
Witham-Fogg, H. G., 13, 15; Works,
 Geranium Growing, 15q.
Woodlice, 151

Yellow spot, 143

Zineb powder, 145

Caption to rear end paper
Ivy-leafed Pelargonium Balcon Rouge
Photo H. Smith